Twinkle

Social Fictions Series

Series Editor

Patricia Leavy (*USA*)

VOLUME 39

The titles published in this series are listed at *brill.com/soci*

Twinkle

By

Patricia Leavy

BRILL
SENSE

LEIDEN | BOSTON

All chapters in this book have undergone peer review.

Library of Congress Cataloging-in-Publication Data

Names: Leavy, Patricia, 1975- author.
Title: Twinkle / by Patricia Leavy.
Description: Leiden ; Boston : Brill Sense, [2021] | Series: Social
    fictions series, 2542-8799 ; volume 39
Identifiers: LCCN 2020046621 (print) | LCCN 2020046622 (ebook) | ISBN
    9789004447066 (paperback ; acid-free paper) | ISBN 9789004447073
    (hardback ; acid-free paper) | ISBN 9789004447080 (ebook)
Subjects: GSAFD: Love stories.
Classification: LCC PS3612.E2198 T95 2021 (print) | LCC PS3612.E2198
    (ebook) | DDC 813/.6--dc23
LC record available at https://lccn.loc.gov/2020046621
LC ebook record available at https://lccn.loc.gov/2020046622

ISSN 2542-8799
ISBN 978-90-04-44706-6 (paperback)
ISBN 978-90-04-44707-3 (hardback)
ISBN 978-90-04-44708-0 (e-book)

PRAISE FOR
TWINKLE

"Remember that wonderful book you read a while back where you imagined that the heroine had more steel in her spine than you got to see? She's back, and this time, the steel is on equal display with the softness we treasured upon meeting her. In this new installment of the story of Tess Lee and Jack Miller, Patricia Leavy gives readers a thrill ride that feels at once tantalizingly fast and thoroughly familiar. Every day is an action sequence when we are healing from trauma. Often, the moments that feel the smallest are the ones that require the greatest courage, and sometimes, enormous threats from the outside wind up feeling small in comparison to what we have already faced within ourselves. With *Twinkle*, Leavy consistently illustrates this essential truth of trauma recovery while delivering laughs and zingers aplenty. In a world where wit is often an underappreciated weapon, this tightly crafted sequel to *Shooting Stars* sparkles brightly and pierces straight to the heart."
Alexandra "Xan" Nowakowski, Ph.D., MPH, Florida State University

"In *Twinkle*, Tess and Jack show us how love of self is what we need to heal and find our strength. Once again, we find Tess struggling with dark shadows until the light of love shines through. Love is like stardust that scatters light into our dark places, illuminating a better path. I cannot wait for the next Tess and Jack novel."
Sandra L. Faulkner, Ph.D., author of *Poetic Inquiry: Craft, Method and Practice*

"Tess Lee's mantra is to change the darkness into light, but we all have things in life that hold us hostage. In *Twinkle*, Patricia Leavy returns to Tess and Jack's love story, and we see how far that mantra can take them as they battle external and internal threats. I love these characters, and I think you will too. *Twinkle* is a captivating read. I

highly recommend this novel for pleasure reading, book clubs, or as supplemental reading in a variety of courses in the social sciences."
Jessica Smartt Gullion, Ph.D., Texas Woman's University

"*Twinkle* picks up with Tess and Jack following the emotional devastation of Leavy's introduction to their love story. Fast paced yet still complex, the reader is presented with the first stages of happily ever after, bringing with it both expected and unexpected problems. Like all Leavy works, this novel serves multiple audiences, from the casual reader to the academic. This is her second novel that offers an exploration of contemporary masculinities, showing the many shades beyond the narrow archetypes we've come to expect in literature. Moreover, *Twinkle* investigates the human cost that our security services willingly pay to keep us safe from the terrors at the edges of our civilization. This is a perfect choice for book clubs and summer reads, but would also be ideal as a core novel in a range of courses from history, psychology, social work, sociology, or women's/gender studies. It could also be used in criminal justice, forensic science, or intelligence studies. Ultimately, *Twinkle* is contemporary literature at its very best, one that hides its lessons inside perfectly baked cookies that leave you feeling better about the world and the people in it."
U. Melissa Anyiwo, Ph.D., Curry College

"We could all learn a lot about compassion from Tess Lee! *Twinkle* is not just a fun sequel for those desperately hoping to spend more time with Tess and her loved ones; it is also a stunning example of love, compassion, empathy, and meaningful relationships that will make you laugh out loud while reminding you about the importance of your loved ones."
J. E. Sumerau, Ph.D., The University of Tampa

"Tess and Jack are back in a book that is romantic, thrilling, and adventurous. Challenged by the question, 'Why not live exactly the life you want?' Tess and Jack explore their greatest hopes and deepest dreads, struggling to be defined by their gifts and not their wounds.

Can we ever truly put our past behind us? If not, how do we weave it into our present and future without being stunted by it? Can we continue to contribute if we reconfigure our lives, re-imagine our work? All these deep questions are embedded in a fast-moving love story that will have you turning pages until you've read the whole book in one sitting. A must-read."
Eve Spangler, Ph.D., Boston College

"Patricia Leavy's psychological thriller, *Twinkle*, peels back the layers of scars caused by childhood trauma, PTSD, depression, and worthiness, and gives the reader a twinkle of hope that one can overcome the worst of the worst, even in dark times. *Twinkle* is not the typical feel-good novel; it is much more. As a clinician and educator, it is often difficult to explain the depth of pain that trauma deposits on a soul, and the residue of that pain that lingers many years later. *Twinkle* provides the depth needed to generate empathy and the insight required to create change. This healing story has made an indelible mark on my soul and I am excited to share it with my students."
Renita M. Davis, LICSW, PIP, Troy University

"For two decades, author Patricia Leavy has assembled a treasure chest of books that use storytelling to demonstrate the promise and peril of human existence and connection. Her latest novel, *Twinkle*, is no exception. Readers will be 'with' Leavy and her characters as they work through issues of loss and doubt, and cope with the impact these issues have on their relational bonds and lives. *Twinkle* is an impressive story that will no doubt compel readers to reconsider their own lives in relationship to the characters' and the relational bonds they maintain (or don't) with others."
Keith Berry, Ph.D., University of South Florida

"Once again, I eagerly sat down with Tess Lee and her interesting life: her beloved Jack, her friends, her politics, her literary career, her experiences, and her grace. Once again, I read with gusto, immersing myself in this appealing world of relationships, compassion, and

creativity, in a kind of experiential healing. These characters and these books, of which *Twinkle* is the latest gleaming edition, explore much-needed themes of kind-heartedness, integrity, courage, chosen family, and the power of the arts to heal, challenge, expand, educate, and connect. The latter is my favorite theme and it emerges throughout this series in important, constant, and powerful gestures of advocacy and education. In these times of global disruption and instability, we need the arts more than ever. Leavy well understands that the arts are transformative and important, and I found myself smiling during those moments in the text when I could hear her scholarly voice coming through powerfully and authoritatively. Leavy is well-versed in these terrains and is an absolute champion of the arts, being a veteran arts-based researcher. *Twinkle* is a shining example of arts-based research. Leavy has always championed the arts in education, and she certainly does so with integrity in this series, through both the telling and the showing, in both the form and the content of this work. *Twinkle* is beautifully written, crisp, and deeply inviting to read. I wanted to stay with the words and with the beautifully drawn and fully formed characters. They are so vivid on the page; it was as if I were in the room with them. I found myself reading late into the night, waking in the wee hours and picking up *Twinkle* again and again. I didn't want to rush my reading either, reluctant to leave the characters, lingering with them for as long as I was able. There are many powerful moments in *Twinkle*, important ethical themes and actions. Leavy's accomplished plotting means that events and stories emerge powerfully and convincingly throughout the book. Like her previous title, *Shooting Stars*, issues of trauma and pain are compellingly and sensitively managed with ethics and grace, written beautifully and offering a comforting and informative experience in the reading, despite the unsettling nature of the subjects. There is so much beauty in *Twinkle* that stayed with me long after I read the last page: the beauty of our good friends, of healing, of real and steady love, of life's experiences wonderfully told. I cannot wait for the next book; I'm so hungry for more."
Alexandra Lasczik, Ph.D., Southern Cross University

"Leavy demonstrates how the residue of the past (e.g., former peers, formative events, gender socialization) can reappear – and sometimes even haunt – present relationships and future ambitions. A vibrant portrayal of insecurity, pain, self-disclosure, healing, and hope; a timely tale of relational time."
Tony E. Adams, Ph.D., Bradley University

For more information, visit the author's website
www.patricialeavy.com

For Melissa Anyiwo
Thank you for loving these characters,
and never doubt that you are enough

CONTENTS

ACKNOWLEDGEMENTS

Thank you to everyone at Brill | Sense for supporting this book and my growth as an author. Special thanks to John Bennett, Jolanda Karada, Els van Egmond, Dan Carney, Caroline van Erp, Evelien van der Veer, and Robert van Gameren. Thank you to the editorial advisory board members of the *Social Fictions* series for your generosity, and to the early reviewers for your kind endorsements. Heartfelt thanks to Shalen Lowell, the world's best assistant, spiritual bodyguard, and friend. Sincere appreciation to Celine Boyle, the world's best writing buddy, for the invaluable feedback. Thank you to Clear Voice Editing for the always phenomenal copyediting services. To my social media community and colleagues, thank you boundlessly for your support. My deep gratitude to my friends, especially Tony Adams, Vanessa Alssid, Keith Berry, Renita Davis, Pamela DeSantis, Sandra Faulkner, Ally Field, Robert Charles Gompers, Alexandra Lasczik, Linda Leavy, Laurel Richardson, Xan Nowakowski, Mr. Barry Mark Shuman, Jessica Smartt Gullion, Eve Spangler, and J. E. Sumerau. My love to my parents. Madeline Leavy-Rosen, you are my light and my heart. Mark Robins, you're the best spouse in the world. Thank you for all that words cannot capture. Melissa Anyiwo, this is for you. Thank you for driving up to Maine to read the first draft of this series and for loving these characters so much. Never doubt that you are enough.

CHAPTER 1

"Thank you, I've got it from here," Jack said to the driver, taking the luggage and seeing him out. He turned to Tess, "Welcome home, Mrs. Miller."

She smiled, removed the lei from around her neck, and placed it on the counter.

"You looked so beautiful running around in the sun. I'm going to miss the leis and the flowers in your hair," Jack said.

"Me too. That was the most incredible vacation I've ever had. Pure paradise. Thank you for making it so special," she replied.

"I still can't believe we never took a honeymoon. What were we thinking? I'm glad we could make up for it for our second anniversary."

"Maui is so beautiful. That house was magical. If we were there right now, we'd probably be relaxing on our private beach or splashing around in the ocean," she said.

"Or making love on the beach. Or on a chaise lounge. Or in the pool. Or in the outdoor shower. Or in every room of the house," Jack said, slipping his hands around her waist. "The way you smelled, the salt water, the coconut oil, the flowers – I'll never forget it. And the taste of pineapple dripping from your lips..." He leaned in and kissed her.

"I never thought it was possible to make love so many times in a day. Somehow, even after two years, you still make each time feel like the first," Tess said.

"That's because I fall in love with you all over again every day, every time I look into your big, brown eyes. I really do."

She smiled.

"I still can't believe the staff caught us by the pool," Jack said, laughing.

Tess giggled. "Well, it was very chivalrous of you to try to cover me up with that towel."

"We should have stayed longer. Ten days wasn't enough. Getting a break from work only highlighted how stressful it is to think about terrorism day in and day out. After years of seeing the worst in humanity, I started to forget that some people live differently."

"I know. You needed a Technicolor break; you've been on the dark side for too long. But I thought it would be nice to spend our actual anniversary in our own home, the same place we got married. Plus, I didn't think you should use up all your vacation time," she said.

"Baby, I'd quit my job and move to Maui if you wanted. I'm serious. We could buy that house."

She smiled. "You'd miss your work."

"I'd get over it," he shrugged.

"And our friends," she said.

"They'd visit."

She looked down. "I don't think I could survive without Omar. It's been him and me since our first day of college."

He put his hand on her face, she looked into his sea blue eyes, and he pulled her close in a comforting embrace. "I know what his friendship means to you. I'm just saying that you can write from anywhere, so if you ever decide that you want to pack up and be a beach bum with me, I'd be all in. And I'm pretty sure that Omar and Clay would make good use of the guest house."

"Maybe if you let me drive the motorcycle or pilot the helicopter next time, I'll consider it," she said.

He laughed. "The idea is to *live*. I think you need a few lessons first, sweetheart. Plus, I loved feeling your arms wrapped around me when we took those sharp bends around the cliffs."

"That was so much fun. I'd never been on a Harley before. You made me feel safe and so free."

"That's exactly how I want you to feel, always, just like I promised you on the day we got married, standing right over there."

"Jack, I love you so much. Happy anniversary."

"I love you with my whole heart. Happy anniversary, sweetheart. Let's go to bed. I'm not done with you yet."

***

When Jack's alarm rang the next morning, he tried to sneak out of bed quietly.

"Hey you, get back here," Tess said.

"Go back to sleep," he whispered.

"I can't," she said, sitting up and stretching her arms. "Omar's coming over for breakfast. We have a lot to catch up on."

"I'm still shocked that you didn't bring your phone to Hawaii. I didn't think you could go that long without texting him."

"He understood. I didn't want anything to interrupt our romantic getaway. Besides, he knew how to get a hold of us if there was an emergency."

"I'm going to hop in the shower," Jack said. "I can only imagine what's waiting for me at the office."

"Okay, baby. I'll make coffee."

"Thank you," he said, leaning down for a quick smooch.

Half an hour later, Tess handed Jack a tumbler of coffee. "Have a great day, baby."

"You know I always miss you when we're not together, but it'll be even worse than usual today," he said.

She smiled. "For me, too."

"Tell Omar I said hello," he said, on his way out the door.

***

"Aloha, Butterfly," Omar said, placing a bag and a manila folder on the counter before squeezing her tightly.

"Oh, I missed you and your gorgeous English accent so much," Tess replied.

"I brought bagels. I was hoping you'd be so blissed out from your tropical sex romp that you'd be willing to eat a few carbs. There's a fruit salad, too, in case I overshot."

She giggled. "I've been really good about my eating, actually. You'd be proud of me. I can't remember the last time I counted my food or purposely skipped a meal. I just feel so content in my own skin now, because of Jack. I don't need to do that anymore, at least not all the time."

Omar smiled. "I'm so happy you're embracing the love you deserve."

She squeezed his hand and said, "I'm trying."

"Okay, so carbs it is. I also brought along a few work things, if you're in the mood. I've been running your publishing empire flawlessly as usual, but I do need to check in with you on a few matters. Come on – you pour the coffee, I'll fix the bagels, and then I want to hear everything. Well, maybe not everything. I do need to be able to look Jack in the eye again."

Soon, they plopped onto the couch and began gabbing. Tess ate half a bagel and gushed about her trip. "The house was marvelous, all one floor, with walls of windows overlooking the ocean. It was remote, up on a cliff. There was a pool and Jacuzzi, a cliffside dining table under a canopy where the staff served our meals, and a heavenly private beach."

"Sounds perfect," Omar said. "Next time, bring me."

"Well, there was a fully equipped guest house."

"Now we're talking," he said.

"We went up in a helicopter, and the view took my breath away. The island is gorgeous, all the bright colors: blues, greens, pinks, and purples. You should have seen Jack piloting. He was in his element; it was super sexy."

"I know how you love a man working a big machine," he said with a laugh.

"You're terrible," she replied, playfully hitting his chest.

"You've always been a bit of a daredevil, my little fearless one, but never thought I'd see the day you rode on a Harley. Bloody hell, Butterfly, please tell me you wore a helmet."

"Yes, Jack made me. It was exhilarating. It pushes all the thoughts and worries out of your mind, and you just feel the air, boundless amounts of air."

Omar smiled.

"The best part was being alone together. Every afternoon, Jack would lie down on a chaise lounge by the pool or on the beach, and I'd sit between his legs and lean back against his chest. He'd wrap his arms around me and we'd watch the ocean for hours, waiting for the sky to turn shades of pink and coral. It was the most serene feeling, just being together, in silence, and feeling that close. I didn't know it could ever be like that between two people, and that's how I always feel with him – like we understand each other entirely."

"I honestly can't believe you came back. It sounds like nirvana; you should've stayed," Omar said.

"Actually, Jack wants to quit his job so we could go live there."

"Jack's a smart man."

Tess raised her eyebrows in disbelief.

"Well Butterfly, why the hell not? You're barely forty years old and you have over five hundred million dollars, not to mention a private jet you barely use anymore. You have the means and ability to live any life you choose. You can write from anywhere."

"But Jack's job is here in DC," she said.

"Jack's been serving his country since he was eighteen years old. That's over twenty-five years. He's served with dedication and honor. He can retire young and enjoy himself. If he wants to work, I'm sure there's a wealth of consulting or specialty work he could do with his experience. Perhaps he could do volunteer work."

"Our friends are here. You're here," she said.

"Butterfly, if you buy an estate in Hawaii, I promise to wear out my welcome in your guest quarters. We've lived in separate cities before, and we always spent more time together than apart. Besides, you don't have to do it full time. You could buy something there and keep this place for vacations, or split your time between the two. You still have the house in Los Angeles in between. Why not get some use out of it? Hell, you could buy homes anywhere you choose. I know you'd love to have an apartment in New York or Tokyo. There's no need to be stuck here all the time. Jack hardly needs to keep doing the daily grind, nor do you. Why not live exactly the life you want? You both deserve to just be happy together. Most people only dream of that kind of freedom. What's stopping you from living your dream?"

She looked down.

"Let's do a little exercise. Without censoring yourself, tell me the things about your life, personal and professional, past and present, that you love."

"Spending time with Jack, with you, and with our friends. Writing, of course. I even liked the book tours, if only they had been shorter and more manageable. I liked traveling to different countries, although I've done enough of that for several lifetimes, so I'm not desperate for it. But all the rest of it – the media and road dog life with events nearly every day – it was exhausting and became too much. You know that. The privacy I have now, I would never want to give up again. A quieter life suits me."

"Butterfly, you could have a life entirely structured around everything you just said. You and Jack can live anywhere, spend all your time together. You could travel where and when you like. Your friends aren't going anywhere, and you know you can't get rid of me. Why not go for it? Jack would be keen on it."

"It's just… Well, it's just…"

Omar took her hand. "I know what you're really scared of, but you needn't be. Jack loves you as much as any man has ever loved anyone. He's not going anywhere. I remember his wedding vows, the commitment he made, and Butterfly, he meant every word."

She smiled, her eyes watery.

"Just promise me you'll think about it. You and Jack can have every happiness, any way you both choose. You deserve that. And you can still write your stunningly inspirational novels and do book events wherever and whenever you like. Jack would always be free to travel with you. Hell, he can be your personal security. Few authors have a former federal agent as their bodyguard. It would be very cool. Besides, it would help me sleep at night to know he's there."

She nodded faintly. "Enough about me. How have you been? What have I missed?"

Omar's expression turned sour.

"Oh no. I recognize that look. What's wrong?" she asked, rubbing his hand.

"Things aren't exactly fabulous with Clay right now."

"What's going on?"

"I met him for lunch at the hospital last week and noticed something between him and some guy he works with. I can't explain it, but there was something going on."

"Did you ask him about it?"

"Not right away. I let it fester for a few days until I thought I was going to implode, so then naturally I confronted him in the worst possible way."

"Good job," she joked.

"I know," he said.

"And? What did he say?"

"He said the man had come on to him, but that he turned him down flat. He assured me there's nothing to worry about, nor would there ever be."

"Then why don't you look relieved?"

"Well, he hadn't told me about it. He kept it to himself."

"Maybe he didn't want to upset you over nothing."

"That's exactly what he said."

"Don't you believe him?" Tess asked.

"I want to believe him, and I mostly do. Clay is honest and I trust him. It's just that there's this small kernel of doubt, and when doubt creeps in, it takes up residence like a squatter. You want it out of your mind, but you don't know how to evict it."

"I understand," she said, leaning over and hugging him.

"I know you do," he whispered.

Tess sat back and said, "I would believe him, though. You two are perfect together. You've built something solid, and Clay would never jeopardize that. Talk to him about it. Talk to him until you're sure."

"You and Jack have only been together for two years, but you both waited so long for love that I think you just knew what to do with it when it came. Clay and I have been together a lot longer. Sometimes I worry that people stop seeing each other over time; you each become like the wallpaper or a piece of furniture. What if he doesn't see me anymore? That might make something new look quite appealing."

"That's just your doubt speaking. Clay does see you. He doesn't want anyone else. But maybe you need to work on things a bit and not take him for granted. I'm sure every couple goes through this. You both have a million things on your plate, but you have to make sure you can see the trees in the forest. Give more attention to the one thing that matters most; give him your undivided, full attention for a while and see if things improve. That's the decision Jack and I made when we got married. That's what we knew to do with our love: prioritize it. We live that choice every day and I'm so grateful we do."

"Thank you. You two make it look effortless, but I know it probably isn't. I know nothing grows unless you tend to it."

"Water your garden and it will blossom," she said.

Omar nodded. "I don't care if you tell Jack, but please don't tell anyone else. I don't want people to act strangely around us."

"Of course."

"I could use more fuel. Let's refill our coffee mugs and then go through this," Omar said, lifting the manila folder. "It's just a few licensing and foreign translation contracts that require your review and signature."

Tess grabbed the mugs and stood up. "That was another wonderful thing about Maui – I didn't have to be Tess Lee. No one wanted anything from me, and I could just breathe the briny sea air. Even the house staff called me Mrs. Miller. It was bliss. I felt totally like myself."

"Butterfly, you can have that any time you want it. Remember, you and Jack don't owe anyone a thing."

She smiled.

"He loves you, Tess. He's completely and madly in love with you and he always will be. There's nothing to fear."

"I'll get us that refill and then you can drag me back into the world of Tess Lee."

CHAPTER 2

That Friday night, Tess, Omar, and Clay scored their usual table at Shelby's Bar. Soon, Bobby joined them without Gina, who wasn't feeling well and stayed home. They were all talking and laughing when Jack and Joe arrived.

"Sorry we're late," Jack said, sliding into the booth next to Tess.

"Well, give me a kiss and I'll forgive you," she said.

He smiled and kissed her. "I actually brought something better."

"Baby, there is nothing better."

Joe threw his arm up and signaled for the waitress to bring a couple bottles of beer.

"How would you like to go to a black-tie gala and dance the night away with me two weeks from tomorrow?" Jack asked.

She furrowed her brow. "What are you talking about?"

"The president is hosting a ball to celebrate international peace and the arts. From what I hear, the guest list will mostly include ambassadors and ministers of art and culture from around the world. A couple of people from each agency were invited."

"Somehow, Jack and I were the two from the Bureau that snagged golden tickets," Joe said, taking a swig of beer.

"It's no accident. Apparently, you're her favorite author. Did you know that?" Jack said.

"I've heard that before," Tess replied.

Omar started laughing.

"What?" Jack asked.

"Butterfly, are you going to tell him, or should I?"

"Oh, hush," Tess said, picking up a pretzel and flinging it at him.

"Tess was invited to the event weeks ago. She declined. Apparently, she didn't mention it to you," Omar said.

Tess picked up another pretzel and chucked it at him.

Omar continued, "I'm actually going to this thing myself, if you can believe it. Abdul and Layla are flying in from Dubai. Since my NIH grant ended, when I'm not helping Tess dominate the world of publishing, I've been assisting Abdul with a series of international arts events he's planning. Clay can't get his shift covered that night, so I begged Tess to come and keep me company, but it turned out she'd received an invitation for the two of you that she had ignored. I never thought she'd pass up a chance to see Abdul."

"If you'd let me get a word in, you'd know I'm not. I was going to invite Abdul and Layla over for dinner," she said.

"Wouldn't it just be easier to go to the big fancy dinner that you're all invited to?" Omar asked, crinkling his nose and tossing a pretzel at her.

"Sweetheart, we don't have to go. But I know how much you love the arts and there's going to be an orchestra. Plus, I thought it would give me a chance to spin you around a dance floor that's a bit nicer than this," Jack said.

"With the beer stains and ubiquitous sticky spots, what could be more charming than this place?" Tess said.

Bobby laughed.

"Why don't you want to go?" Jack asked.

"I do want to. I didn't want to go as Tess Lee, but I'll happily go as Tess Miller. Count me in. I'll be your plus one. I can only imagine how sexy you'll look in a tux." She turned to Omar. "Work your magic and try to get us seated together, pretty please."

"Only if you promise to behave. No sitting on the floor in front of the president," Omar chastised with a chuckle.

She flung another pretzel at him, but he ducked and it bounced off Clay's head.

"Oooh, sorry, Clay," Tess said.

"Quite all right, but now you have to tell us what he's talking about."

Tess shook her head.

"Actually, it's one of my favorite memories of you, Butterfly," Omar said. "I just like to tease you."

She shot him the side eye.

"This must be good. Tell us," Bobby said.

"It's actually a very sweet story," Omar said. "It was about eight years ago. Tess was invited to a gala in London to raise money for children's art programs. Your typical, not-so-typical star-studded event, swarming with royalty. She dragged me along."

"Uh, you begged me to take you. Clay, don't be offended, it was before he met you, but there was some duke or prince or something that he was dying to meet. He practiced his curtsy for weeks," she said, erupting into laughter.

"It was a bow and I'll get you for that, Butterfly," he said, tossing a pretzel at her.

Everyone laughed.

"Mockery is a two-person sport," she quipped.

"Anyway, Tess wore the most spectacular gown. It had a big hoop skirt, very Cinderella, and her hair was styled in long, spiral curls with little rhinestones sprinkled in. We were chatting with a potpourri of royalty when a little girl who was there with the charity came over. She tugged on Tess's arm and said, 'You look like a fairy princess.' So of course, Tess knelt and says, 'So do you, my dear. Can I tell you a secret?' With wide eyes, the little girl nodded. Tess said, 'I have some fairy dust. Would you like to see it?' Naturally, the girl said yes. Tess took her hands and they sat on the floor together, right in the middle of this gala. She opened her purse and pulled out a small tube of gold glitter. She sprinkled some into her hands and blew it in the air. You should have seen this little girl; she couldn't stop grinning. Tess sprinkled some glitter into the girl's hand and blew on it. It wasn't long before they both had glitter in their hair, on their faces. They sat there doing that over and over again, as if they were in their own private snow globe. Honestly, it was one of the sweetest things I've ever seen."

Tess blushed. Jack leaned over and pecked her on the cheek.

"What did the people around you do?" Joe asked.

"Well, they sure as hell weren't going to get on the floor with her. Everyone was so formal at this thing; I think they were stunned. But it was so precious, and it's Tess Lee after all, so they didn't quite know what to do. Eventually, Tess stood up and carried on with the conversation as if nothing had happened." He turned to Tess. "That really is one of my favorite memories of you, Butterfly."

She smiled.

"And they couldn't have been too affronted, because one of those royals fell madly in love with her that night. He pursued her relentlessly."

"You never told me that," Jack said.

"There's nothing to tell. I turned him down."

"Yeah, and he couldn't quite believe it. No one turns down royalty," Omar said.

"Trust me, it can be done. I can't imagine spending even a moment with a man who won't sit on the floor in the middle of a gala to make a child smile. Besides, he didn't fall in love with me, he was only mildly charmed for a fleeting moment."

"Uh, he was absolutely in love with you," Omar replied. He turned his attention to Jack. "Well, you heard it from her lips. Be warned, Jack. For all we know, she'll lie on the floor in front of the president and make snow angels."

"Ooh, that's not a bad idea," Tess jested.

"That's fine with me. I'd happily join her," Jack said. "I'll be the luckiest man there with her on my arm."

She leaned over and kissed him softly.

"Well, that's enough of story time. I want to dance. Clay, are you ready for a whirl?" Tess asked.

"Definitely," he replied.

Tess and Clay excused themselves to the dance floor. Jack looked over at Omar. "Why did Tess turn down the invitation?"

"She'll know just about everyone there from the fifteen years she spent relentlessly traveling the world. She's very influential and beloved in the world of the arts, not to mention that she'll probably have the highest net worth of anyone in that room many times over, which never fails to draw attention. She wields a certain kind of power you haven't really seen yet. She's this petite, angelic thing, but she is truly powerful. People are drawn to her. Plus, she's bloody gorgeous and has that Tess factor. I don't have to tell you. People love her, and somehow that doesn't sit well with her."

"Yeah."

"You've seen her do a couple of book signings, but this is a whole different level. She had decided to leave that world before you two met, and then after you married, I think she felt there was no place for it in her life anymore. I'm not sure, really, but she's different since she met you. The people at these things always want something from her, and she can't help herself but to oblige them. It's never just a carefree night of dancing. Despite what she says, you know she can't really go simply as your wife. When she's in that type of setting, she's Tess Lee, whether she likes it or not."

Jack nodded. "I know. I love her as she is; she's the only one who has a problem with it."

"Being there with you may make it feel different for her. Maybe she can finally enjoy one of these soirees. Although I should warn you, many of her past admirers will be there. I hope that won't bother you."

"I can handle it. I know what we have. It's hard to blame anyone for wanting to be with Tess."

"If it helps, she never had a real interest in any of them. She's never looked at anyone the way she looks at you."

Jack smiled and turned to look at Tess twirling around on the dance floor. He caught her eye and she returned his smile. He asked Omar, "Was that royal really in love with her?"

"Completely."

CHAPTER 3

The next morning, Tess and Jack were snuggling in bed. Jack was playing with Tess's hair and teasing her. "I'm serious," he said. "You'd look good in a tiara; maybe you should have gone for that royal."

"First of all, everyone looks good in a tiara."

"*That's* your first of all?" he said, tickling her mercilessly.

She giggled uncontrollably until he stopped.

"Okay, I should have said, 'In no particular order.' But my other points were that royalty is absurd, and that man was dull and uptight. And furthermore, Omar is out of his mind. He wasn't in love with me."

"Well, that's where you lose all credibility. I trust Omar on this one. It's impossible not to fall for you."

She slid her hand behind her head, pulled out her pillow, and walloped him in the face.

"You did *not* just do that," he said through laughter.

"That's what you get for saying such silly things," she said, now lying flat on the bed.

"Hey, I'm just grateful you'd give up a crown and palace for a guy like me," he said.

"Jack, there are no guys like you. There's only you."

He leaned over, caressed her face, and kissed her.

"Give me my pillow," she said.

"Oh, now you want it back?" he teased, holding it in his hand as far away from her as he could stretch. "You're gonna have to come and get it."

She started to crawl over him when his cell phone rang. "Ah, you're in luck," he said, handing her the pillow. "It's Bobby."

"See if they want to go to the movies with us later," Tess said, propping herself up against her pillow. "If Gina's there, we can persuade you two to see a romantic comedy and not one of those killing spree monstrosities."

Jack laughed and answered the phone. "Hey, Bobby. What are you guys up to later? Save me from a chick flick."

"Jack, something's happened. We just got back from the hospital. Gina had a miscarriage."

"Oh my God, I'm so sorry," Jack said. "Is she okay?"

"Physically, she's fine. Just a little pain. But she's devastated. Everything I say seems to make it worse. She wants to see Tess. I don't want to impose, but…"

"Hang on," Jack said. He covered the phone and turned to Tess.

"What's wrong?" she asked.

"Gina had a miscarriage, and she's asking for you. They were hoping we'd come over."

"Of course," Tess replied, springing up. "I'll jump in the shower. Tell him we'll be there in an hour."

***

"Thank you so much for coming," Bobby said.

"Where else would we be?" Tess replied, hugging him.

"I'm so sorry," Jack said.

"Come on in," Bobby said, directing them to the living room sofa. "Can I get you guys something to drink?"

"I'm fine, thank you," Tess said.

"Me too," Jack said.

"We weren't really trying, we had just decided to stop *not* trying, you know? We didn't even know she was pregnant. She didn't feel well last night and then she started having terrible pains and she was bleeding. I took her to the emergency room, and that's where we found out. Gina couldn't stop crying. She's just wrecked. I keep trying to focus on good things. They said there's no reason we can't try again. Gina's perfectly healthy and this just happens sometimes. So, I keep telling her we'll just try again. Everything I say is wrong. It's just making her more upset. I didn't know what to do. I asked if she wanted me to call her parents or any of her friends. She said, 'Tess. I only want to see Tess.' I didn't want to bother you, but…"

"Nonsense," Tess said, rubbing his hand. "We're always here, whatever you and Gina need."

Bobby's eyes started to tear. Tess leaned over to hug him, and he held her tightly.

"I feel so bad. She's in so much pain and I just want to make it better."

She rubbed his back. "I know. She needs to feel this pain, but it will get better. It just may take a little time."

Bobby pulled back, sniffled, and said, "Thank you. She's in our bedroom. She'd love it if you went to see her."

"Of course," Tess said, standing up.

"Tess, thank you," Bobby said.

She smiled and walked away.

"How are you holding up?" Jack asked.

"I can't believe this is happening. Gina's a mess and I feel totally useless. I can't even process what's happened because I'm so worried about her."

Jack put a hand on his shoulder. "Maybe she'll feel better after she talks with Tess."

Bobby said, "Tess is the best."

"Yeah, I know."

"She's the only person Gina wanted to see."

Jack smiled.

"The funny thing is that when we first met Tess, Gina was so starstruck that she thought it would be impossible to become friends. It took her a little while to get over that. Once you know Tess though, you'd never guess how successful she is and what her time is worth. She's so down to earth and she's always there for her friends, like we're more important to her than whatever other demands she has on her time. It's crazy when you think about what she's achieved."

Jack smiled. "Her priorities are pretty clear."

"And she's so damn sweet; she always knows how to make people feel better. It's like a gift," Bobby said. "Do you remember when we found out about Joe's cancer scare and that he had asked Tess to go with him to see the oncologist?"

Jack nodded.

"I asked him why he brought Tess instead of telling us. He said, 'Because she's the kindest person I've ever met, and I was hoping some of that good energy would rub off on me.' I totally got it."

"She kept his secret, too. She never told me a word about it."

"He told me that having her there was like placing a halo around a dark cloud. She made him focus on the light."

"That sounds like her," Jack said.

"I hope she can do that for Gina," Bobby said.

***

Tess knocked gently on the bedroom door.

"Come in," Gina said.

Tess opened the door to find Gina sitting in bed, tissues strewn all around her. She looked at Tess and started crying.

Tess leaned down and hugged her, whispering, "I'm so sorry." She sat on the edge of the bed and took Gina's hand.

"It hurts so bad. You were the only person I wanted to see, the only person who I knew would understand."

"They don't call me the people's high priestess of pain for nothing," she said with a smile.

Gina laughed through her tears. "That doesn't bother you anymore?"

"I've learned to roll with it," Tess replied.

"Bobby thinks I'm mad at him," Gina said.

"He just feels badly that you're hurting, and he doesn't know how to help."

"Can I ask you something personal?"

"Anything," Tess replied.

"Have you and Jack ever thought about having children?"

"We talked about it. In the end, we decided that it had taken us so long to find each other that we really just wanted to focus on our relationship."

"I've wanted kids my whole life. I always played with dolls. I treated them like they were real – changing them, dressing them, feeding them. I never left the house without my favorite one. I imagined someday they would be real. I think that's why I became a teacher, just to be around kids. Did Bobby tell you we didn't even know I was pregnant?"

"He did."

"Tess, how can losing something I didn't even know was there hurt so much?" she asked, more tears flowing. Tess held her hand and let her get it out. "I mean, I have this whole body and then the smallest little part of it disappears and it's all I can focus on."

"I haven't had this experience, but I do know what it's like to feel pain and loss, and what it feels like when your body betrays you. It's very dark."

"Exactly," Gina said, wiping her face with a tissue. "I know Bobby means well, but he wants me to look on the bright side. He keeps saying things like, 'We can try again,' and... and..."

"And you need to feel this loss first."

"Yes," she said, bursting into tears. "I wish he understood."

"Tell him how you feel. He's crazy about you. If you tell him what you need, he'll be there for you. I'm sure it hurts him, too. He's just trying to make it easier for you."

"Tess, will you just sit with me for a little while?"

"As long as you want. And Gina, I know you're not ready to concentrate on it, but Bobby is right. Once you grieve this loss, you will see light on the other side. I have no doubt that one way or another, you will have a house full of kids if that's what you want."

"But this one will always be missing."

"I know," Tess said. "You'll learn to live with their absence. The hurt will never go away, but it will become easier to carry."

Half an hour later, Tess walked into the living room. Bobby jumped up. "How's she doing?"

"She's sad, but she'll get through this."

"Everything I say is wrong and just makes her cry more. I'm only trying to cheer her up," Bobby said.

"I know you are. But she needs to mourn this loss. She needs to grieve. It would be better if she were grieving with you instead of alone. Bobby, I know you don't want to see her in pain, but she's already in pain and the only way out is through. She needs to feel this. The more you help her feel it, the easier it will be for her to move through it. This kind of loss can't be glossed over. Grief can't be rushed. Do you understand what I'm saying?"

"Yeah, I think I do."

"Grieve with her, no matter how difficult it is. That's what will help her. That's all she wants."

"Okay. Thank you so much, Tess," he said, hugging her tightly.

"Go to her now, but remember that we're only a phone call away. I'll come back any time, so please don't hesitate," Tess whispered in his ear.

Jack pulled his keys out of his pocket.

Bobby let go of Tess and she said, "Oh, and when we were on our way here, I placed an order with that Italian restaurant Gina loves. It will be delivered in about an hour. It should be enough food for a few days, so that's one less thing you have to worry about."

"You're the best. Thank you."

"Bobby, you will get through this and she will be all right. Just grieve," Tess said.

***

Tess and Jack got home after one o'clock. "Sweetheart, we haven't eaten a thing today. We could go somewhere. What do you feel like doing?" Jack asked.

Tess looked up, her eyes flooded with sadness.

"Oh, sweetheart, come here," he said, wrapping her in a firm embrace.

"I just feel so badly for Gina. She's in a lot of pain."

"I know, but you helped her."

"I didn't do anything."

"Yes, yes you did," he said, kissing her forehead. "There's a reason our friends always come to you when they're in a dark place."

"Because I know pain so well," she said.

He shook his head. "Because you know how to move through it and transform it into light. I love that about you more than you could possibly know. It's very special. It's changed the way I see everything."

She smiled. "Thank you, baby. How about we stay home today? We can cook, get cozy on the couch, and watch a game or something. Nothing would make me happier than just being with you."

"Sounds perfect."

***

"It smells good," Jack hollered. "You sure you don't need help?"

"You helped plenty. Just watch the game. I'm ladling it out now, but it will need to cool for a bit. If you're starving, we have hummus and veggie sticks."

Just then, the doorbell rang.

"You expecting someone?" Jack asked.

"No. Do you mind seeing who it is? The bread is under the broiler and I don't want it to burn."

Jack answered the door. "Hey, Omar. Come on in."

"I'm sorry to just drop by like this. I was passing by, and…"

"You're always welcome, you know that," Jack said.

Tess was pulling the herbed bread out of the oven when Omar said, "Hello, Butterfly."

She looked over and her face lit up. "What a nice surprise! You're just in time; we made lentil soup. You can join us."

"Can I get you something to drink? A beer, maybe?" Jack asked.

"Oh, I don't want to intrude," he replied.

"You're not," Tess said.

"Absolutely. Stay, hang out with us," Jack insisted.

"All right. A beer would be great. Thanks, Jack."

"So, how did I get so lucky to see you today?" Tess asked.

"It's just, well…"

"Oh, dear. I know that look. What's wrong?" Tess asked. She hurried over, still wearing her oven mitts.

"I'm having a mini-meltdown," he replied.

She hugged him and he held her as if he would never let go. Eventually, they parted and she threw the oven mitts on the counter. "What's going on?"

"Clay's working a sixteen-hour shift today, so I stopped by the hospital to bring him one of those wraps he loves from that cute little sandwich shop. I wanted to spare him from that dreadful facsimile of food they serve in the cafeteria."

"That was sweet," Tess said.

"Yeah, well, when I got there, one of the nurses told me he was in the lounge. I headed straight there, and when I opened the door, I saw him having coffee with that guy, the one who hit on him. They were standing there together, holding those pathetic Styrofoam cups. You'd think doctors would be more concerned about the environment, but…"

"Then what happened?" Tess asked.

"He didn't see me, so I bolted."

"Seriously?"

"I panicked."

"Oh, sweetie, they work together. They were standing in their workplace lounge, not lying in bed in the on-call room. They probably just bumped into each other or were talking about a patient or something. It hardly sounds like you caught him having a secret rendezvous."

Omar shook his head. "I know. I can't believe I did that. What's wrong with me?"

"Plenty. Shall I make a list or summarize?" Tess said with a giggle.

Omar smiled.

"I really don't think anything's happening between Clay and that guy. Just last night when we were dancing, he was talking about you and saying the sweetest things. He's hoping to get time off soon. I think he's looking forward to some romantic couple time."

"Really?" Omar asked with a hopeful smile.

Tess nodded. "He told you nothing has or will ever happen with that man. Clay is honest. He's never given you any reason to mistrust him."

Omar took a swig of his beer. "I'm behaving like a child, aren't I?"

"Well, I don't want to kick you while you're down," Tess said with a giggle. "Come on, we're just about to eat. Take a load off in the living room. We've made lentil soup. A friend sent me a recipe for a quick version."

"Let me guess – a rock star? A prime minister?"

"An actor I was friends with when I lived in LA. I won't say who, but you used to have a huge crush on him. Come on, go sit. There's too much bread. You can help Jack polish it off. After we eat, we can get to that list of all the things that are wrong with you. Jack can help."

Omar laughed. "Thanks, Butterfly. You always know what to say."

"I do my best."

CHAPTER 4

Jack was waiting for Tess in the living room when he received a message that the driver to the gala was outside. He knocked on their bedroom door to check on her, calling, "Hey, sweetheart, are you ready?" She opened the door. His jaw dropped and he put his hand on his heart. Tess was wearing an off-white gown with a full skirt and plunging neckline. The entire gown was adorned with crystals. "Almost ready, honey. I just have to put my necklace on," she said, picking up the gold heart locket she had worn every day since Jack gave it to her.

"Here, let me do that," he said. She swept back her dirty blonde hair, he kissed her neck, and fastened the chain.

She turned to him and said, "You are the most handsome man I've ever seen."

"You are so beautiful. You took my breath away," he said. He kissed her softly. "Shall we go?"

"Jack, I need to talk to you," she said anxiously.

"The driver's waiting. Can we talk in the car?"

"Sure."

As soon as they got in the car, Jack's phone rang. "It's the office. I just need to make sure everything's okay."

She nodded and watched as he answered the call.

He covered the receiver and said, "There's a situation and they need my input. I'll try to make it fast."

"It's fine," she replied, fidgeting.

As they pulled up to the gala, Jack was still on the phone. He noticed that Tess was nervously tapping her fingers on her leg, so he quickly wrapped up his conversation and hung up. "I'm sorry, sweetheart," he said. "You wanted to talk to me." He took her hand and realized she was shaking.

"We're here," the driver announced.

"We need a minute, please," Jack replied. He turned to Tess. "Sweetheart, what is it?"

"It's nothing. We should go in."

"Sweetheart, you're trembling. Tell me."

She turned to him and he caressed her face. "Jack, will you please do something for me without asking why?"

"Yes."

"When we leave this thing tonight, let's not talk, let's not say a single word. Let's just go home and make love and be us. No words. Please."

He leaned forward and gently pressed his lips to hers. "Okay."

"Thank you."

Jack told the driver they were ready but that he was going to get the doors himself. He stepped outside, opened Tess's door, and extended his hand. She took his arm and they walked up to the entrance. Photographers hollered, "Tess Lee, over here," and asked them to stop for a few pictures. They posed in the light of the flashbulbs, and then Jack said, "Shall we, Mrs. Miller?"

***

As soon as they were inside, they paused to take in their exquisite surroundings. "Wow, this place is really something," Jack said, admiring the ballroom that featured parquet floors and high ceilings dripping with crystal chandeliers.

Tess smiled.

Jack rubbed her fingers. "Look how pretty the tables are; they're overflowing with white flowers and candles, just like you love," he said. "And the orchestra is in full swing. I can't wait to spin you around the dance floor." She smiled. A waiter in a white jacket passed by, carrying flutes of champagne, sparkling water, and bite-size morsels, so Jack grabbed a sparkling water and handed it to Tess.

"Thank you, honey," she said, taking a sip.

People immediately noticed Tess and offered respectful smiles and nods. She did the same in return. Jack spotted Omar and Joe standing together.

"Butterfly, you look stunning," Omar said, hugging Tess.

"You look absolutely radiant," Joe said, leaning in to peck her on the cheek.

"Thank you. You both look as dashing as ever. Are Abdul and Layla here yet?"

Omar shook his head.

"Please tell me you finagled us seats together," Tess said.

"Uh, well, Butterfly, that's a funny story. Take a deep breath. The short version is that we're all sitting at the president's table."

"So, we're flying under the radar like I asked?" Tess joked, handing her glass to a passing waiter.

"Well, it seems that she's desperate to meet you and had planned to seat you and Jack at her table. When I spoke with the event coordinator to try to get us at the same table, I was informed that, and I quote, 'The president would be delighted to sit with Ms. Lee and her guests.' She wanted to speak with Abdul anyway. They've video conferenced. She's recently become quite interested in his counter-extremism initiative. So, this should be fun! Right, Butterfly?"

Tess rolled her eyes.

"Not bad, Tess. I guess Jack and I should stick with you. Seems you can teach us a few things," Joe said.

Tess feigned a smile and looked down. Jack grabbed her hand and whispered, "Are you okay?"

Before she could answer, a couple walked over. With a thick French accent, the woman said, "Tess Lee, this is a thrill. We're big fans of your work."

"Merci c'est très gentil," Tess replied.

"Ah, you speak French beautifully. It's wonderful that you're here. You do so much to support the arts," the woman said.

"Eh bien ce soir, je suis juste ici en tant que rendez-vous avec mon mari." She turned to Jack and said, "I was just telling them that tonight I'm here as your date."

"Bonsoir," the woman said.

"Bonsoir," Tess replied, and the couple walked away.

"You speak French?" Jack asked.

Before she could respond, she was again interrupted. "Tess Lee, I don't believe my eyes," a willowy man said in a British accent. "You are a vision," he continued, leaning in to kiss her on each cheek.

Tess recoiled and latched onto Jack's arm. "Hello, Oliver. Lovely to see you. This is my husband Jack, our friend Joe, and I believe you know Omar."

They all exchanged polite greetings, and Oliver refocused on Tess. "You've turned down my last three invitations, or should I say, your assistant has. I can't even get a hold of you."

"I'm sorry, I've been busy. Remember when writers used to spend their time writing? Well, I'm trying to bring that back."

He chuckled. "You always were ahead of the curve. Come to London and we'll throw a bash in your honor. I won't take no for an answer."

"I'm afraid you'll have to. I really don't do events anymore."

"But you're here tonight, so there's hope," he said.

"Simply to dance with my husband," Tess said, intertwining her other arm around Jack's.

"I'm sure he won't mind if I cut in. Perhaps I'll convince you when we're on the dance floor. See you later, Tess. You are ravishing. Gentleman," he said, before sauntering off.

Tess leaned over to Jack and whispered, "If you let him cut in, I'll divorce you."

Jack laughed.

"Who is that guy?" Joe asked.

"He's an insufferable little man..." But before Tess could continue, Eliza Elkington tottered over, throwing her arms in the air. "Tess Lee, in the flesh. I've been wanting to do a profile on you for years. I talked my way into an invite to this thing as the date of some German cultural attaché. He's an absolute bore and I hope he doesn't think I'm going to sleep with him. Between us, the most he can hope for is a blow job, and I'd have to be plenty drunk for that."

Jack covered his mouth to mask his laughter.

"Anyway, it's all worth it now that I see you're here, Tess."

"Hi, Eliza. Nice to see you. This is my husband, Jack, and these are our friends. Eliza is the publisher for a women's magazine."

"Not a women's magazine, *the* women's magazine, darling. Well, you certainly married yourself an attractive man," she said, looking Jack up and down dramatically. "Maybe you'll take me for a ride around the dance floor," she said, batting her eyelashes.

Jack smiled politely. "Actually, I'm hoping to spend the night with my beautiful wife."

"Isn't he delicious, Tess?" Eliza gushed. She turned back to Jack. "Good luck keeping Tess to yourself. She's always in demand."

Tess looked down.

"Listen, I'm serious about the profile. We could make it a cover story. I'd love to spend a couple of days in Tess Lee's world, observing, interviewing. I know you're impossible to get, but I do love a challenge and I never take no for an answer."

Tess smirked.

"Promise me you'll think about it," Eliza said. "I'll get in touch with your assistant. Ta-ta!"

Tess smiled and Eliza sauntered off.

"She's enthusiastic," Jack said.

"That's one word for it," Tess replied.

They both laughed.

"You certainly are popular, Tess. It must be tiresome," Joe said.

Tess sighed.

"Butterfly, you didn't really think you could just be Tess Miller, did you? Still, that doesn't mean you can't enjoy yourself with your handsome, and dare I say, sought-after man. What will you do if he dances with Eliza?" Omar said, laughing.

"I'd pay good money to see that. It would be like dinner theater," Tess replied.

"If you let her cut in, I'll divorce you," Jack said.

"She'd eat you alive," Omar joked.

They all laughed.

Just then, the president walked into the room with her chief of staff. The group watched as she shook hands with several people before making a beeline over to them. "Tess Lee, this is an honor," she said, outstretching her arm.

"The honor is all mine, Madam President," Tess said, shaking her hand.

"I'm such a huge admirer of your writing and what you've done for the arts, women in business, libraries, I could go on and on. And you're a self-made woman to boot. I'm delighted we'll finally have a chance to chat. I've been trying to meet you for ages. You're harder to pin down than I am," she said with a laugh.

Tess blushed. "I believe you've met Jack and Joe, and this is my dear friend, Omar."

"Very nice to see you all," she replied. "Omar, I've seen your name on emails regarding Abdul's project. It's good to put a face to the name. My husband is out of the country on business, so Charles is accompanying me tonight. It never hurts to have your chief of staff at one of these things; it's so hard to remember everyone."

They all smiled.

"Madam President, Omar tells me that you've taken an interest in Abdul's counter-extremism project. That's wonderful," Tess said.

"Yes, it's a bold initiative. Several European countries have already stepped up to the plate. I wish I could raise more support for it in other parts of the world."

"Hmm, I see," Tess muttered. "Madam President, I hope I'm not overstepping, but may I ask you a question?"

"Please do," she replied.

"The G8 summit is only weeks away, and if one is to believe the news, terrorism will be at the top of the agenda. And you're hosting this gala, ostensibly for the arts and peace, with ambassadors from the Middle East as well as the G8 players in attendance. It hardly seems like a coincidence."

Everyone looked intently at Tess and the president.

The president smiled and glanced at Charles, who chuckled. She turned back to Tess. "I always knew you were brilliant. I told Charles on our way over here that I've just been dying to meet you. Yes, you're right. I was hoping to build some bridges for a broader counterterrorism initiative. The arts seemed like a, shall we say, gentle way to do that. It's been impossible to bring Japan to the table. I wanted to have the Japanese ambassador seated at our table, but was told that just getting him to say hello to Abdul would be an impossible feat. It goes both ways. They're being quite stubborn. It's turned an otherwise jovial occasion into something a bit more stressful."

Tess smiled. "I see. Who's representing Japan at the gala this evening?"

"Ambassador Kaito Harada," she replied. "He's here with his wife and a few of his aides."

Tess scanned the room. Omar winked at her and they covertly exchanged conspiratorial smiles. Just then, Abdul and Layla arrived, walking straight over. Everyone exchanged warm greetings.

"Madam President, it's an honor to finally meet you in person. Thank you for your support," Abdul said.

"Likewise," she replied.

He turned to Tess and embraced her lovingly.

"I'm so happy to see you, Abdul," Tess said. "Layla, you look stunning."

Layla smiled.

"I've missed you, my light. We are very glad to see you," Abdul said. "Although I must confess, I was surprised when Omar informed us you would be here. I thought you'd given up this life for the simpler pleasures you enjoy."

Tess smiled. "I'm making an exception tonight. Jack was invited, and you know how I love an orchestra."

"I see," he replied.

"Well, shall we find our table?" the president asked. "Tess, you're sitting next to me. We have so much to talk about."

Tess looked at Jack, who smiled and whispered, "You're so damn smart." He squeezed her hand and they headed to the table.

***

Tess was seated between the president and Jack, across from Abdul, their table in the center of the room and directly perpendicular to the band. Tess and Jack engaged in their own conversation about how pretty the flowers were and how divine the orchestra sounded, staring lovingly at each other, Jack rubbing Tess's arm. Waiters came over, introduced themselves, and promptly served drinks. The eclectic group made small talk.

"Layla, how was your trip?" Tess asked.

"Very good, thank you. We stopped in Paris on the way," she replied.

Tess smiled. "Abdul, were you looking at venues for the Paris events? Omar told me a little about it."

He nodded. "We have summits scheduled in Paris, Cannes, Milan, Venice, Frankfurt, London, Cambridge, Toronto, Vancouver, Abu Dhabi, Dubai, and several in the United States. It's become a much larger project than we could have imagined. The participating countries have all donated generously, each underwriting all of the expenses for the events."

"Omar and Tess mentioned something about counter-extremism events," Joe said. "What exactly are you planning?"

"We have designed a program that uses the arts to counter extremism and promote peace. We're hosting week-long summits in cities across the world over the next five years. The participants will include leaders, policymakers, religious figures, artists, military personnel, scholars, and citizens from various walks of life. Each group will be carefully curated. We've been laying the groundwork for many years."

"That's remarkable," Joe said.

"It truly is," the president said.

Abdul smiled. "It has been the effort of many." He turned his attention toward Jack. "You must know that Tess inspired this project, yes?"

Jack looked at Tess with an inquisitive expression and placed his hand on her thigh. "I had no idea, but I can't say I'm surprised."

Abdul smiled. "Yes, I first had the idea when I read her fourth novel, *The Island*, years ago."

"Of course," the president said. "That's one of my favorite books."

Joe smiled. "I should have realized. I love that book."

Abdul continued, "But her influence did not end there. We spoke about it and she suggested how I might make it a reality. She contacted her network and worked her magic to line up the resources and key players."

Tess shook her head. "Abdul flatters me. I really didn't do anything."

Abdul laughed. "I see some things never change."

"You know what hasn't changed? How much I love to dance, and as I recall, you are quite light on your feet. If Layla wouldn't mind…" Tess said.

"He would love to dance with you," Layla said.

Abdul smiled. "With Jack's permission."

Tess rubbed Jack's hand and he said, "Of course."

Abdul extended his hand and Tess rose to meet him. The group watched as they made their way to the far side of the dance floor. Tess stopped right in front of Kaito Harada's table. She looked at him and bowed her head almost imperceptibly. When the song ended, Kaito Harada stood up and approached Tess and Abdul. They exchanged words and the two men shook hands. "Well, I'll be damned," Charles said. "Madam President, are you watching this?"

"I sure am."

Tess began dancing with Ambassador Harada as Abdul strolled back to the table.

"I see Tess knows Kaito Harada," the president said.

"Tess knows everyone; she is very loved," Abdul replied. "She helped Mr. Harada with an art education initiative in Japan years ago, and she is always his personal guest when she does book tours in Tokyo."

"I told you Tess would know just about everyone here," Omar said to Jack.

They all watched as Tess and Kaito danced, engrossed in conversation. When the song ended, someone on Kaito's staff approached to speak with him. Tess headed back to the table. Jack stood up and pulled her seat out for her. "I'm sorry, baby," she whispered.

He lifted her hand to his lips, kissed it, and winked at her, and they both sat down.

She slowly took a sip of her sparkling water and placed the glass back on the table with great care, then turned to Jack and said, "Have you ever been to Japan?"

"No," he replied.

"Tokyo is one of my favorite cities in the world and Kyoto is enchanting, especially during fall foliage and the spring bloom. I would love to go there with you."

"I would love that."

She squeezed his hand and turned to Abdul. "Abdul, the president mentioned you have been in negotiations to bring Japan on board. Wouldn't it be wonderful to have them participate in your project?"

The president and Charles shot each other a look. Everyone eagerly waited at the edge of their seats for the response.

Abdul smiled. "Yes. We tried, but we could not get them to commit. There are other politics at work that they refused to table. The negotiations went poorly and we were deadlocked. I was disappointed."

"Kaito and I just spoke. I explained how important the program is and outlined all the reasons that it would be in their best interest to join. He agreed," she replied. "They are willing to commit to cooperative events in Tokyo, Kyoto, and Osaka, following your model."

Everyone's eyes widened.

"That's wonderful news, Tess, but there must be a price to pay. We offered many things during the negotiations and it was never enough. What must we surrender?" Abdul asked.

"Nothing," she said. "There's just a small gesture. It's nothing, really."

Abdul raised his eyebrows skeptically.

"All you have to do is get up and walk over to him. You must be the one to extend yourself."

Abdul looked down and let out a heavy sigh. "You know what you are asking."

"I know what it signifies to Kaito, but I also know the kind of man you are." She lowered her voice. "It's meaningless. Remember who you are. See this place for what it is. This is only the realm of the

1 percent. Nothing that happens here matters. There is only darkness and light, and love is the bridge between them. Your program is love. Think of the 99 percent to which you've devoted your life. Do you know what I see when I look around this room? Many men who have abandoned everything that once mattered to them for the chatter, for the false trappings of the elite. It's heartbreaking," she said, a tear falling down her cheek. "This gesture," she paused, crinkled her nose, and whispered, "it's meaningless."

Everyone sat with bated breath, the president's eyes glued to Abdul.

"Thank you for your counsel, Tess," Abdul said.

Tess smiled faintly and lowered her chin. "Of course."

A moment passed as Abdul thought quietly. "I would like to take your advice, but how do I know that Mr. Harada will follow through if I make the journey to him?"

"It would be my pleasure to personally escort you and Layla."

Abdul turned to the president. "Madam President, I hope you will excuse us for a moment."

"Certainly," she replied.

Abdul and Layla stood up. Tess whispered to Jack, "I'll be right back." She walked over to Abdul and linked her arm with his. The three approached Kaito, who stood and extended his hand as soon as they arrived. Jack, Joe, Omar, the president, and Charles watched with their mouths hanging open.

"Holy mother of God," the president said. "If I hadn't seen it with my own eyes..." She turned to Jack. "Do you have any idea what your wife has just done? She's extraordinary."

Jack smiled humbly. "Yes, she is."

A few minutes later, Tess excused herself and turned back toward her table. En route, several people stopped her to chat. Jack couldn't take his eyes off her, a slight smiled etched onto his face. Eventually, she made it back to the group. "I'm sorry, baby," she whispered as he pulled her seat out.

"Don't be," he said.

When she sat down, everyone looked at her, their mouths agape.

"It's done. Japan is in. They're making plans, and it turns out Layla and Kaito's wife have quite a bit in common. Perhaps they'll all become friends," she said.

"Well done, Butterfly," Omar said, raising his glass.

"It was nothing," she replied. "Although I don't understand why you didn't just ask me to make a call from the outset."

"Abdul insisted we leave you out of it," Omar replied.

"That's curious," she replied.

"Tess, I consider myself a master negotiator but I've never seen anything quite like that. You certainly live up to the legendary tales I've heard. How on earth did you manage that, let alone in the ten minutes we've been here?" the president asked.

"Kaito is quite old fashioned when it comes to gender roles. I'm sure you're used to dealing with men like that, Madam President."

Everyone laughed.

"I knew that if he saw me, he'd feel obligated to ask me to dance. That was my chance to have them shake hands and exchange pleasantries as a courtesy to me. When I was dancing with Kaito, I had the perfect opportunity to bring up Abdul's project and explain why I thought it was in his country's best interest to participate. He values my opinion. He's not a man who is willing to give something for nothing, but I explained the need for equity for the program to work. Of course, he demanded a gesture, a show of power. Kaito operates from a hierarchical notion of respect, hence forcing Abdul to make the journey to him."

"What about Abdul?" Joe asked. "What was all of that about the 1 percent?"

"Abdul cares more about peace than politics. He wanted to say yes, but I had to give him a way to live with it. Although it was merely symbolic, it was still a concession. Abdul and I used to study different religious texts and mysticism when we were touring the Middle East. In some regions, our lives were constantly under threat and we were literally trying to take the guns from people's hands and replace them with paint brushes, pens, and books. Abdul needed spiritual guidance. We read quite a bit about Kabbalistic thinking. One thing we could both agree on was the notion that everything we see in this realm – these flowers, those candles, the designer gowns, and the necks dripping with diamonds – it's only 1 percent of what there is in the universe. Our souls exist in the 99 percent, so we must not become distracted by the frills of this superficial, material realm."

"You're brilliant, Tess," Joe remarked.

She shook her head. "You're very kind."

"He's right. You led him exactly where you wanted him to go," Charles said.

She looked at him sharply. "No, I would never do that. I led him exactly where *he* wanted to go. It has nothing to do with me." She turned to the president. "Now I hope you can enjoy your evening without the added stress you mentioned earlier."

"Is that why you did all that?" she asked in disbelief.

"Jack and Joe have devoted their lives to fighting terrorism and this program will diminish the need for that work. It will make the world a little safer. It was also good for both Abdul and Kaito and those they represent, and you, after all, are our host. Sometimes things are in everyone's best interest, if we can only recognize that," Tess replied.

"You are a wise woman," the president said.

Tess blushed. "Madam President, I hope you don't find me rude, but my husband promised me a night of dancing, and so far, it's all been with other men."

They all laughed. "Certainly, please enjoy yourselves," the president replied.

"That's my cue," Jack said. He rose, took Tess's hand, and led her to the dance floor. He placed his hand on the small of her back, pulled her close, and said, "You are breathtaking and I love you beyond words."

She smiled. "Let's just dance."

***

Tess and Jack danced for ages. Several men asked to cut in, but Jack politely said, "I'm sorry, not tonight." Finally, they rejoined their group, holding hands and smiling at each other like two people in on a private joke. As they sat down, the first course was served.

"Thank you, Jerome," Tess said to the waiter. "This looks nice," she said to Jack, admiring the red and golden beet salad.

"I made the pumpkin recipe you gave me, Tess," Layla said. "It was delicious and so aromatic."

"Oh, that's one of my favorites. I'm glad you liked it. I can't take credit; I got the recipe from a friend in Afghanistan."

"Yeah, that friend just happens to be the president of the country," Omar said.

"No, it's his brother. He's a lovely man and a wonderful cook. I know his brother is a bit more, um, complex," Tess said.

Joe laughed. "That's diplomatic."

"You don't have normal friends," Omar said.

"You're right. I have you," she quipped.

Omar rolled his eyes playfully. He then turned to Charles and Joe and engaged them in conversation.

The president focused on Tess. "Do you like to cook?"

"Yes."

"That's one thing I miss. I used to love cooking, and especially baking. I found it so relaxing, a way to decompress and sort through my thoughts," the president said.

"I suppose you don't have time anymore," Tess said.

She shook her head.

"What do you do for pleasure?" Tess asked.

The president sighed. "The two things I loved were reading and baking. I still manage to read. I never miss a Tess Lee novel."

Tess smiled. "I can only imagine the demands on your time and that you feel obligated to use it for the benefit of others, but perhaps it's also important to do things that are restorative. I can recall countless reports of former male presidents playing golf, tennis, fishing, or even surfing. I'm sure you have an incredible kitchen at the White House. I hope you can give yourself permission to use it."

The president smiled. "Thank you, Tess. I actually miss having girlfriends to sit around the kitchen with, make a pot of coffee, and bake cookies. Of course, we never talked about bake sales, more like foreign policy and funding for the arts, but that was the way we did it. The people I know in Washington aren't really those kinds of friends."

"I suspect it's hard to have those types of relationships once you're in your position. Everyone wants something from you, even just to be near you," Tess said.

"Indeed. I imagine that's something we share in common. No one warns you about the loneliness, do they? You can be surrounded by admirers and yet feel totally isolated. I guess we should be grateful to be too busy to think about it," the president replied.

Tess smiled. "Oh, I don't know. I thought that for a long time. But at some point, perhaps it's good to pause and make sure that we are powering the rocket and not just holding on for dear life."

The president let out a huff. "Yes, perhaps. Now tell me, what you love most is writing, yes?"

"Since I was a girl."

"Your novels are sublime. You can capture the balance of pain and hope in our lives like no one else. When I need courage or inspiration, I read your work."

"That's very kind," Tess said.

"I've noticed that you use the same dedication in each of your books, since your debut novel. You always write 'to everyone, everywhere.' That's lovely."

Tess smiled.

"What's your creative process like?" the president asked.

"It's different every time. That's why I'm still in love with writing. Sometimes, I get a complete idea, like a movie unfolding before me. Other times, I just have a character that I can see and hear. Sometimes, I know the last line and I write my way to it. It never happens the same way twice."

The conversation continued and soon the salad plates were cleared. The band resumed playing.

Joe approached Tess and said, "I know Jack wants you all to himself, but I would love to steal a dance with you."

"There's no need to steal what I'll happily give you," she said, rising and taking his hand.

Omar turned to Jack. "I'm going to stretch my legs. Want to head to the bar for a real drink?"

"Sounds like a plan."

Once at the bar, Omar threw back a shot of vodka.

"You okay?" Jack asked. "You don't usually drink very much."

"Can I ask you something?" Omar replied.

"Sure."

"If a woman hit on you, no, if a woman propositioned you, would you tell Tess?"

"Listen, it's just a matter of how much you trust Clay. For what it's worth, I really don't think he's the type of person to cheat."

"But what would you do if a woman came on to you?" Omar pressed.

"I'd shut it down in a way that was crystal clear. Would I tell Tess? If there was something funny about it that I thought we could laugh at, sure. Otherwise, probably not. I wouldn't see any reason and there'd be no point upsetting her."

"Thanks. I know you're right, it's just my insecurity talking. Clay is… Oh, shit. Incoming," Omar said as a man made a beeline toward them. "Thank God I did that shot. This guy makes my ears bleed. Jack, whatever he says, please stay calm."

Jack looked at him for an explanation but there was no time.

"Omar, well I'll be damned. Great to see you," the man slurred in a southern drawl.

"Hi, Dick. What brings you here?" Omar replied.

"Hang on, I need a refill." He turned to the bartender. "Top it off. Bourbon."

"You sure you need another?" Omar asked as Dick grabbed his drink so forcefully it sloshed about in the glass.

"Ah hell, I need something to get through this night. You know the company donates a shitload to the arts for the write-off."

"How touching," Omar muttered.

Dick took a swill of his drink. "Bernard Bentley told me you got him mixed up in some international project. You should have come to me."

"And why is that?" Omar asked.

"My bank account's bigger," he said, erupting in laughter. He composed himself and continued, "Don't worry about me; I got a girl back at my hotel for later, the kinda girl who does what you say. But I'll tell you, man to man, I'd drop her in a flash if you could get me a night with Tess. Hell, Tess can have me for as long as she wants, and I don't say that about most women, course most women ain't worth as much as I am. That Tess, she's such a tiny little thing, but I'd love to bend her over and…"

"And let me just stop you right there and introduce you to Tess's husband, Jack Miller."

"Well no shit, Tess tied the knot."

"Uh, yes she did. Jack is a federal agent. Basically, he's spent the last couple of decades killing people, professionally."

Dick burst into laughter. He stuck his hand out, "Dick Clayton. Good to meet you. Hope there's no bad blood. I've had a hard-on for Tess for years. Didn't know she got married."

Jack carefully placed his glass on the bar, stared daggers at the tactless buffoon, and softly said, "Don't speak that way about my wife or any woman ever again." He turned to Omar and said, "I'm going back to the table."

"Coming right along with you," Omar said. "Goodnight, Dick. Have fun with your hooker or whatever. Try to avoid getting arrested."

On their way back to the table, Omar said, "I'm very impressed that you didn't pummel him."

"It wasn't easy, but I didn't want to cause a scene. Who was that asshole?"

"Oil tycoon. Tess only knows him because he buys his way into events like this. She uses her extensive network to raise money for the arts and literacy, including from his company, always putting the cause above all else. She can't stand him."

When they got back to the table, Jack sat down. He put his hand on Tess's back, leaned over, and said, "I just met Dick Clayton."

"I'm so sorry for you. Which did you find more repellant: his arrogance or his misogyny?"

He laughed.

"At least he's well named. If ever there was a dick," she said.

He kissed her cheek and said, "Sweetheart, I need to feel you in my arms. Would you like to dance?" Before she could respond, a man approached the table.

"Excuse me, Madam President. I hope I'm not intruding," he said.

"Not at all," she replied.

He turned to Tess. "Are you Tess Lee?"

"Yes," she replied.

He smiled brightly. "I am so humbled we can finally meet in person. I am Ebo, Pireeni's colleague. We have exchanged many emails."

Tess jumped up and hugged him like an old friend. "I'm so glad to meet you. The work you do is incredible. Ebo, this is my husband, Jack." They shook hands, and she introduced him to the group. "Ebo works with several orphanages in Ethiopia. He created an arts and literacy program for the children there."

The president stood up and shook his hand. "That's very commendable."

Everyone echoed the sentiments.

Ebo turned to Tess. "If I may, I wanted to show you photographs of what you have made possible. You must see the children with their books and the art projects they have created. It has been life changing for them." He slid his phone out of his pocket and started scrolling through pictures. Tess started to tear as she watched the photos whiz by. "They're amazing," she sniffled.

"I do not wish to disturb your evening any further," Ebo said, pocketing his phone. "I'm grateful for the chance to thank you in person."

"Thank you for all that you do," Tess said, clasping his hands.

Ebo said goodbye and walked away. "Sweetheart, are you okay?" Jack asked.

"I just need a minute," she said. "Please excuse me," she said to the group and dashed out of the ballroom.

"Jack, what was that about? He thanked her," the president asked.

"I don't know," he replied. He sat down and turned to Omar.

"Tess funded the entire program, every penny. It was meant to be anonymous. She doesn't like attention for these things, so you probably shouldn't say anything when she gets back."

"Wow," Charles muttered.

"I'll say," Joe mumbled.

"Is Tess all right?" the president asked.

"Tess does much good in the world, but she does not like to dwell on it. When she is forced to contemplate what she has done, she does not think about the children she helped, only the ones she cannot help. She feels the suffering of others deeply. It has made her a gifted writer, a perceptive analyst of the human condition, one who knows that the shadow side of pain is hope, as you suggested, but there is a grave personal cost," Abdul said.

Jack stood up. "Please excuse me." He walked out into the lobby and waited outside the restroom. When Tess emerged and saw him, she smiled and softly said, "Hey."

"Hi, sweetheart. May I have this dance?"

She nodded, a tear falling from her eye.

"Oh hey, come here," he said, enfolding her in his arms.

***

"That was delicious," the president said, as the waiter cleared the dinner plates.

"Thank you, Jerome," Tess said as her plate was removed.

"Tess, you hardly ate a thing. How was the eggplant?" the president asked.

"It was fabulous, thank you. I'm just not very hungry."

Jack took her hand under the table, brushing his fingers against hers.

"How long have you been vegetarian?"

"Since I moved away from home when I was nearly eighteen. I just can't bear to hurt living beings."

The president smiled. "That's interesting, given what Jack does for a living. Certainly not that he wants to hurt anyone, but the nature of his work."

"Sometimes the world requires us to do things we'd prefer not to do, so we sacrifice some part of ourselves for the greater good and we try to find a way to live with it. That's something I understand," Tess replied.

"You understand too well," Abdul said. "I hope someday you understand less."

Jack brushed the side of Tess's face. She leaned into it and looked into his warm, blue eyes. "I love you," he mouthed.

"I love you," she mouthed in return.

The president was about to say something when the waiter interrupted. "Excuse me, ma'am," he said to Tess. "A gentleman asked me to deliver this to you." He handed her a note. She read it and said, "Thank you, Jerome. Where is he?"

The waiter pointed across the room. She peered over. The man held up his glass and smiled. She raised her glass and smiled in return. "What is it?" Jack asked. She handed him the note, which read:

Rumor has it your husband won't let anyone dance with you. I wanted to say hello. M.

"Who's M?" Jack asked.

"Mikhail Petrov, Russian minister for the arts. He's a special friend. You'd like him; he tells the dirtiest jokes I've ever heard."

"Is he here with his goons?" Omar asked, craning his neck to look.

"He never goes anywhere without personal security," Tess replied.

"Oh, and I see he brought Svetlana. That explains why he's bored and passing you notes like in grade school," Omar said.

"She's not that bad," Tess replied.

"Butterfly, have you ever tried having a conversation with her? She couldn't find Russia on a map."

Everyone laughed.

"Perhaps she has other charms," Tess said. "I like Mikhail."

"I never trust a man who travels with personal security and whatever Svetlana is," Omar rebuffed.

Everyone snickered.

"But this does explain a strange conversation I had earlier," Omar said. "Serge approached me and asked about you and Jack."

"Well, that's irksome. What did he want to know?" Tess asked.

"Just how serious you two are," Omar replied. "Relax, I told him you're madly in love and that it's going to last forever. Now I realize he was inquiring for Mikhail. Seems he's still in love with you."

"Oh please, you're ridiculous," Tess replied, as she reached for Jack's hand under the table.

"Tess, you've certainly led an extraordinary life. I can only imagine the stories you could tell," the president said.

"Actually, I think I've only recently gotten to the good part," she replied, rubbing her fingers against Jack's. Jack smiled as they looked at each other out of the corners of their eyes.

"I've met Mikhail a couple of times, but I can't say I have a good sense of what kind of man he is," the president continued.

"He cares about the arts and culture, but corruption surrounds him. Personally, I've always gotten on very well with him. He can talk about philosophy and poetry for hours, he's hilariously funny, and he drinks like a fish," Tess said.

"I'll give you that, Butterfly. I don't know how he was still standing after doing all those gruesome cherry vodka shots in that bizarre little bar. It really did look like a brothel."

Tess giggled. "It did. That's the night I tried smoking a cigar. God, that was dreadful."

"Butterfly, I told you not to inhale."

She shrugged. "It was fun. You must admit, Mikhail knows how to entertain."

"Plus, he did nearly kill a man for you. I guess if you're willing to forget how bloody scary that was, one could almost view it as gallant," Omar said.

"Oh hush, he did no such thing," Tess protested.

"I'm telling you, if that man walked out of there alive, he was probably missing a few fingers," Omar said.

Tess shook her head. "You're overly dramatic."

"What happened?" Jack asked.

"We were in a private room in a Moscow bar with a smattering of diplomats, ambassadors for the arts, and so on. You know, Tess's usual, utterly surreal group of friends."

"They weren't friends," Tess argued. "They were acquaintances."

"Some man from Mikhail's outer circle had too much to drink and tried to get a little too friendly with Tess. Mikhail, inebriated and blinded by his feelings for her, almost killed him. First, he nearly broke his hand, or quite possibly did. Then, he threatened him. It was all in Russian, so I don't know exactly what he said, but that man was scared for his life. Then, Mikhail had his goons remove him. I'm telling you, he never made it home, certainly not in one piece."

"I'll admit that things got a little heated, but everyone settled down and it was fine. I really think they just asked that man to leave. Let's not get distracted with stories about Mikhail's drunken escapades. More importantly, did you and Abdul try to get Russia on board with your project?" Tess asked.

"That's even funnier than watching Svetlana try to read a map," Omar replied.

Joe and Charles cracked up.

"It isn't possible. They would never work with us," Abdul said.

"Really?" Tess muttered. She turned her attention to the president. "Madam President, now that Russia is back at the G8 table, wouldn't it be wonderful if they signed on to Abdul's project? Then you'd have all the players working cooperatively on something. That could only mean positive things for diplomacy in general."

"I'm afraid I agree with Abdul. It's not possible. Even if we could get them interested, which is beyond a long shot, I can only imagine what they'd try to strong-arm us out of in return."

"Abdul, do you remember when we were touring the Middle East and we approached that check point crawling with armed men? Our security insisted they would make us turn back," Tess said.

Abdul laughed. "You truly have not changed. Yes, of course I remember. You are right. One should never give up before they have tried."

"Honestly, I think you're all right and that they'll say no, but isn't it a conversation worth having?" Tess asked.

"What are you thinking?" Charles asked.

"I don't know. Mikhail will speak with me, but I'd need to brainstorm what to say. You're all quite right – they have no interest in working with any of you, no offense."

Everyone laughed. "You are candid, Tess. A woman after my own heart," the president said.

Tess smiled. "There would have to be a new angle, a motivation we haven't considered yet. The biggest problem is that he doesn't have autonomy. He won't make a single move without first getting clearance from above. He has the Russian president on speed dial. Mikhail is smart; he understands the implications of using his budget and influence to do anything international. It's just after ten here, which means that it's just after six in the morning in Moscow. That's workable, at least."

"Butterfly, he won't do this just because of his feelings for you."

Tess rolled her eyes. "Of course not, but he will listen in earnest to what I have to say."

"I admire your determination, but it really can't be done," the president said.

"You're probably right, but it seems worth a few minutes of our time to be certain," Tess replied. She turned to Jack. "What do you think Russia truly wants at this moment? It's not peace, it's not cooperation with the West, and it's certainly not freedom or funding for the arts."

"Power," he said. "They want power."

"Yes. And power is different from capital. Wealth is flashy, but power…"

"Power conceals itself," Jack said.

"Exactly, you're brilliant," she said, leaning over to kiss him. "Honey, I need to speak with you privately," she said softly. He leaned closer and she whispered, "Mikhail and I had a very brief thing. It didn't mean anything to me, and it was ages ago. I think of him as a friend. I can only have this conversation with him if I go alone, but if it makes you uncomfortable, I won't. Would you mind?"

"Of course not. I trust you implicitly," he replied, stroking her cheek with the back of his hand.

She pulled a pen out of her purse and wrote something on the back of Mikhail's note.

"What did you write?" Jack asked. She handed him the note, which read:

I have a proposal for you. Meet me at the bar. Leave your thugs behind. Tess.

Jack smiled.

"Butterfly, before you do this, please answer one question I've always been curious about. You're right that Mikhail is smart and knows how to have a good time, qualities one should never undervalue. But I know how discerning you are; there's something else you like about him. What is it?" Omar asked.

She smiled. "Remember when he hopped on the jet and traveled the Baltic States with us?"

"How could I forget? That book tour became nothing but bars and night clubs. I had dark circles under my eyes for weeks. It was fabulous."

Tess giggled. "When we stopped in that little gelato shop in Riga, he ordered a scoop of vanilla. When you take all of this away, that's who he really is. And that is why we understand each other. He will hear what I have to say, even if we have to do the dance for the benefit of others."

Omar chuckled. "I understand."

Tess put her hand up to signal for a waiter. "Jerome, please deliver this to that man." She watched Mikhail as he read the note. He laughed, held up his glass, and smiled.

"Ah, he laughed. He's in a good mood," Tess muttered.

Mikhail got up and meandered over to the bar.

"Even if this is futile, I really must say hello to him anyway. Please excuse me," she said. As soon as Tess left, Jack turned to Omar. "Is he really in love with her?"

"Since the moment they met. You'll see. But he also respects the hell out of her."

Jack watched as she glided over to the bar, looking like a princess, her gown sparkling under the light of the chandeliers. Mikhail picked her up and dramatically spun her around in the air, paying no mind to the dozens of inquisitive eyes. Then, he put her down and kissed her on both cheeks. They leaned against the bar and began talking.

"I don't understand," the president said. "What was all of that about vanilla ice cream?"

"That's Tess-speak for 'he keeps things simple.' That's why she likes him. It's her favorite quality; it goes hand in hand with honesty," Omar replied.

Jack smiled.

"Brace yourself, Jack. This could take a while. I once watched the two of them debate a minute aspect of Nietzsche's work for hours. I was like, 'Bloody hell, I'll just Google it,' but they preferred to spar," Omar said, sipping his wine.

"Who won the debate?" Jack asked.

"Tess did, and I'm not really sure how. Mikhail and the others were all hell-bent on their perspective. It got absurdly heated. Russians take this stuff so seriously. I could see that Tess had enough of it. She leaned over and whispered something to him. He turned bright red, laughed, and declared that Tess was right."

Jack laughed.

"Your wife really is something," the president said.

"Yes ma'am, she is," Jack replied.

"If anyone can do this, it's Tess. I have seen her accomplish the impossible before," Abdul said. "She has rare talents. It's interesting because the American media portrays her as quite complex, but I have always thought the opposite. She has a decidedly simple, uncluttered perspective about the world and people. Do you agree, Jack?"

"Yes, I do. You know, on the day of our wedding, Tess told me you are one of the only people who really understands her."

"She is extremely dear to me. Tess has two very special gifts. Her first gift is her ability to witness people. I could point out that

49

she is the only person at our table to call our waiter by his name this evening. She sees everyone."

They all looked down, huffed, and smiled.

"Her second remarkable gift is story. People cannot understand how she is so talented in both the arts and in business, but it is just those two gifts. In tandem, they explain both her literary and business prowess. She truly sees people and knows how to reach them. Then, of course, is the purity of her singular motivation: love. People know that when they speak to Tess, there is no other agenda. She sees only darkness and light, and she doesn't care about politics or power. She never lies. There is no manipulation. Whatever she is saying to him right now, I promise you she believes it. There are no games. This is why people trust her so unreservedly. With all due respect, Madam President, it is the reason why no politician could broker this deal, but why if anyone can, it is Tess."

They watched in stunned silence. "Madam President, are you seeing this?" Charles asked. "He just pulled out his cell phone. He's making a call."

"Unbelievable," Joe muttered.

They tried not to stare as Mikhail spoke on the phone for several minutes, becoming increasingly animated. When he hung up, he and Tess continued talking. She leaned over, whispered something to him, and he nearly fell over laughing. Then, he took her hand and led her to the dance floor.

"Well, this is going to make Svetlana's head explode," Omar joked. "She's always been hugely jealous of Tess. Everyone knows he's hung up on her."

Jack let out an audible huff. "I can see that, but I can hardly blame him."

They all watched as the two whirled around the dance floor. Mikhail said something to Tess and she laughed hysterically. At one point, she turned to Jack and winked. He smiled. When the song ended, they walked over to the table. Everyone stood up to greet them.

"Madam President, it's a pleasure to see you again," Mikhail said.

"Likewise," she replied, shaking his hand.

"Omar, nice to see you," Mikhail said.

"It's been too long, Mikhail. We were just talking about that wild little bar you took us to in Moscow."

Mikhail smirked.

Tess introduced everyone else. "Abdul," she said, "since you and Mikhail will be working together, I wanted you to have a chance to meet." After chatting for a few minutes, Mikhail said, "I better get back."

"Yes, it seems your date is waiting for you," Tess replied, glancing over at Svetlana, who looked like she was breathing fire.

"Oh, please," Mikhail said. "I'm going to the bar."

Tess laughed.

Mikhail turned to Jack. "Many men would cut of their hands to be with your wife."

"Or someone else's hand," Omar muttered. Tess shot him a look of admonishment and Joe muffled his laughter.

Mikhail continued unphased. "You are a lucky man, Jack. Congratulations." He said goodnight to the group and walked off.

Tess blushed. Jack brushed the hair away from her eyes and whispered, "He's right about one thing: I am the luckiest man in the world."

They all sat down. Tess coolly took a sip of her sparkling water and finally said, "As you heard, they're in."

The president's eyes were like saucers. "I'm speechless. What have we given them?"

"Nothing. It certainly wasn't my place to give them anything," Tess replied. She looked at Abdul. "They'll host events in Moscow and St. Petersburg. It's not perfect; there will be a fair amount of censorship regarding the participant list and content, but that was inevitable. So, expect that they'll be modifying the program quite a bit."

Abdul grinned from ear to ear. "How can I thank you?"

Tess shrugged. "It was nothing. Abdul, you know the types of connections I have. Why didn't you and Omar use my name or ask for my help? I would do anything for you and your cause."

His expression turned solemn. "You are always generous, but I know that what you seek is not in this room. I did not want to drag you back into the 1 percent. Tess, my light, please hear these words as I heard yours earlier: you deserve that which you seek. Do not feel that you must sacrifice any part of yourself. You have already given so much."

Tess looked down. Jack caressed her hand.

"I don't understand, Tess. How did you make this happen without major concessions in return?" Joe asked.

"I kept it simple. I agreed with Jack that they want power. But of course, they don't want to be viewed as the brutes that much of the world thinks they are. This program, if viewed as a public relations strategy, solves a deeply rooted image problem. Mikhail took my point and was able to convey it up the chain of command. In that light, we are offering them an opportunity. Mikhail is pragmatic. Besides, I did him a favor years ago and I think he was pleased to repay it."

"Well, I don't know what to say. Tess, you've been my favorite author for so long and I was hoping to impress you tonight, but it's been just the opposite," the president said.

"Madam President, you are already impressive. You needn't try, it's self-evident."

"Good. Then I'm hoping you might come and visit me one day. Perhaps we can make a pot of coffee, bake some cookies, and discuss foreign policy or funding for the arts. I would love to be your friend," the president said.

"I would be honored," Tess said.

"See? No normal friends," Omar said with a chuckle.

They all laughed.

Dessert was served, meringues filled with lemon curd and dripping in berry sauce.

The president stood and said, "I've had such a wonderful time with all of you that I've neglected to make the rounds. There are many people I must say hello to. Please excuse me."

Jack put his hand on the small of Tess's back. "Sweetheart, would you like to dance?"

She nodded. "Desperately."

On the dance floor, Jack said, "So, you took him on your jet? Should I be jealous that he picked you up and twirled you around?"

"He just did that to piss off Svetlana. You should never be jealous of anyone or anything. You are the most incredible man in this or any other room, and as I told him, you are my everything."

"I know, I just wanted to hear you say it."

She looked at him intently.

"He's in love with you."

"Oh please, you've been spending too much time with Omar," she rebuffed.

"I saw the way he looked at you. It's undeniable."

"That's it, you and Omar can no longer play together."

He laughed. "Okay, we can talk about someone else who loves you: the president."

Tess smiled dimly but her expression turned forlorn. "Honey, I'm sorry if tonight wasn't what you hoped for. I feel terrible. I wanted to help Abdul, and all the people here know me, and it's impossible to…"

He leaned in and kissed her. "You have nothing to apologize for. Let's go home, Mrs. Miller. I have a promise to keep."

CHAPTER 5

Tess leaned against Jack in the limo and he absentmindedly massaged her fingers, not a word spoken. When they got home, Jack followed Tess to the bedroom, taking off his jacket and tie on the way. She sat down at her vanity, unfastened her necklace, and slipped off her heels. Jack took off his cummerbund, unbuttoned his shirt, and kicked off his shoes. Tess stood up and turned around. He unzipped her gown and helped her step out of it. She turned to face him. In a faint voice, she said, "Jack, if you…" He grabbed her, held the back of her head, and swept her into a frenzied kiss. She unzipped his pants and pulled them down. He picked her up and she swung her legs around his waist. He carried her over to the bed, lay her down, and they made love passionately. After, they lay looking at each other, kissing, as Tess ran her fingers along the scars on his body.

"Tess, I love you so much."

"I love you, too."

"You were spectacular tonight. I was in awe. Do you have any idea how proud I am of you?" he said.

She looked down.

He wrapped his arms around her. "I'm afraid you think you can't be all that you are and still be with me. I can handle it. I don't want you to give up anything."

"I know."

"Or is it something else? I saw the look in your eyes when Abdul spoke."

She just looked at him.

He brushed his lips lightly against hers.

"Jack…"

He tipped her chin up to look in her eyes. "Do you remember that day in Hawaii, in the outdoor shower, when I took you from behind?"

"Yes, it was incredible."

"Do you remember what I whispered?" he asked.

She nodded.

"I said, 'Don't let me hurt you.'"

"Jack, you could never hurt me."

"Not on purpose, but I needed to know that you would tell me if it was too much, that you can tell me anything. Otherwise, I never could have been with you like that, so intensely. Tess, there's such deep trust between us. You can tell me anything. I want to know what's going on in your mind. I know you're not ready to talk about whatever it is that's bothering you, but I'm here when you are. Someday, I hope you'll choose to tell me how you feel and what you need in the moment. I promise then that we'll be as close as two people can be."

Her eyes filled with tears. "I'm closer to you than I've ever been to anyone."

"I know, and that's how I feel about you, which is why I hope that someday you'll know in your heart that it's okay to tell me what you need. You never ask for anything for yourself, but you can and you should." He wiped a tear away and pressed his body into hers. "Let's fall asleep just like this," he said, and he kissed the top of her head.

***

The next morning when Tess woke up, Jack's side of the bed was empty. She brushed her teeth and wandered into the kitchen.

"Hey, sweetheart. I was just making some coffee," he said, spooning grounds into the filter.

"Jack," she said softly.

He turned toward her.

"When I was growing up, I felt like I was buried alive. I couldn't breathe. Writing allowed me to take in gasps of air. It kept me from suffocating."

He put the spoon down and looked at her tenderly, giving her his full attention.

"I was barely twenty-two when I became well-known. Fame threatened to turn writing into something else. I had to struggle to keep it for myself, my only means of air, just that one part of my life. Everything else, I gave away willingly. I only kept that one thing for myself. When you're famous, nobody sees you for who you are. It makes it hard to breathe. When I met you, I felt like you saw me entirely and I saw you, no secrets, no masks. It was like oxygen. After surviving on gasps for so long, I was suddenly flooded with air. Jack, how we see each other, what we have, it's everything to me. It's literally the air I breathe. You, writing, and our friends are what's real to me, what keeps me above ground. Last night, the way people saw me and what they wanted from me, it's not that you can't handle it, it's that I don't want it, but more than anything, I don't want you to see me through their eyes. And I feel guilty because I know that being Tess Lee is a privilege I should use for others, but I just want something for myself. I just want to be. I just want to breathe."

Without a word, he walked over, cupped her face, and kissed her. He gently placed her head on his chest, wrapped his arms around her, and held her for a long moment before whispering, "Thank you."

"I love you," she said.

"Tess, I love you with my whole heart, forever, exactly as you are. You don't have to do anything. Just be."

CHAPTER 6

The days and weeks passed uneventfully after the gala. Tess wrote, Jack worked, and they spent all their free time together. Tess called Gina every day as she moved through her pain toward healing. Sometimes, Bobby texted or called Tess to ask for advice, which always made him feel better. Omar and Clay continued to work on their relationship. When they were all together on Friday nights, Tess noticed that the couple seemed increasingly at ease with each other, holding hands and looking at each other with love.

The president was true to her word and invited Tess to the White House residence. Tess was happy to oblige.

Jack came home from work one night with Joe in tow, who they frequently had over for dinner since his girlfriend broke up with him.

"Hi, Joe. It's always good to see you," Tess said, hugging him.

"Thanks for having me," he replied.

"Hi, sweetheart," Jack said, handing her a bouquet of white hydrangeas.

"They're so beautiful. What's the occasion?" she asked, kissing him.

"I don't need a reason other than wanting to see you smile."

"All you have to do for that is walk through the door."

"I'll put them in a vase," Jack said.

"Something smells good in here," Joe said.

"I'm afraid I can't take credit. I was running late from Kate's, so I had some eggplant rollatini delivered. I'm keeping it warm in the oven while I throw a salad together."

"Who's Kate?" Jack asked.

"Oh, I mean the president. She insisted I call her Kate when we're alone. I don't blame her. It's hard to become friends with someone when you call them by their title, especially that one."

"You saw the president today?" Jack asked, placing the flowers on the bar.

"Uh huh. I guess I forgot to mention that she called. It seems she wanted to take my advice and allow herself some 'me time.' She invited me over to bake cookies. She made a pot of coffee and we just gabbed away while the cookies were in the oven."

Jack and Joe exchanged a look.

"What?" Tess asked.

"Well, sweetheart, not everyone hangs out socially with the president."

"Nor do they call her Kate," Joe said with a chuckle.

Jack laughed, handed him a beer, and took a swig of his own.

"Like I said, she insisted I call her Kate. She's an amazing woman. I really enjoy her company."

"What did you two talk about?" Jack asked.

"Literature, mostly. She's extremely well read. We also talked about funding for the arts, spirituality, all kinds of things. I think she just wanted someone to hang out with who doesn't want anything in return. As it turns out, we have a lot in common. She said she felt like I was an old friend, and I felt the same. We made the most scrumptious cranberry orange cookies. They're her family recipe, passed down for generations."

"You ate a cookie?" Jack asked in disbelief.

"I had two."

He looked at her wide-eyed.

"Well honey, she *is* the president."

"I thought she was your friend, Kate?"

"I can hold two thoughts," Tess replied. "Anyway, the cookies are delicious. She insisted I bring some home for you and Joe, so save room."

Jack smiled.

"Next time, we're making chocolate chip. I told her they're your favorite."

"Next time?" he asked.

"She invited me back a week from Thursday, you know, assuming she doesn't have some kind of emergency that demands her attention, which could always happen."

Joe chuckled.

Jack kissed the top of her head and smiled.

"What?" she asked.

"Nothing. Just be you."

The following Thursday, Jack was in his office reviewing a case with Joe and Bobby when Tess called to see if she could stop by. When she arrived, she knocked on Jack's door.

"Come in," he said.

She walked in holding a plastic container. "Hi, honey."

"Hi, sweetheart," he said, standing to kiss her. "This is a nice surprise. To what do I owe the unexpected pleasure?"

She placed the container on his desk and walked over to hug Joe and Bobby. "Well, I was driving by, on my way home from the White House. We made too many cookies and I didn't want them to go to waste, so I thought I'd drop them off for all of you."

"Thanks," Bobby said, opening the lid.

"There's dark chocolate chip and milk chocolate chip with walnuts, Jack's favorite," Tess said.

Joe grabbed a cookie. "It's not every day I eat something the president made."

"Hey, I made them too," Tess said.

They all smiled.

"Anyway, I know you need to get back to work, but I wanted to know if we're free Sunday night. Kate's just dying for us to meet her husband. I invited them over to our place, but it's such a nuisance for her to be followed by the Secret Service that we decided it would just be easier if we went there. Did you know she's never had mac and cheese with butternut squash? I couldn't believe it. Her cook will make a salad and we'll bring the macaroni. I guess there's some policy about her food needing to be tested, but I'll just make extra."

Jack stared at her, his mouth agape.

"What now?" she asked.

"Uh, well, sweetheart, it's just unusual having dinner at the president's residence."

"Being the president is her job, it's not who she is. She's a human being just like everyone else, and I happen to really like her. Are we free?"

"Uh, yeah. Sure," he said.

"Great. Don't worry. It'll be casual. Just wear jeans." She leaned over and gave him a quick peck. "I should let you all get back to work. Share those cookies with everyone," she said on her way out the door.

Jack looked at Joe and Bobby, their open mouths covered in cookie crumbs. "So, I guess I'll be going to the White House to have dinner with the president of the United States. And I'll be wearing jeans and carrying a casserole dish."

They all erupted into laughter.

Several weeks later, the entire group met at Shelby's for their regular Friday night get-together. Jack, Joe, and Bobby told the group about a recent terrorist threat they had thwarted, and it was clear that work was taking a toll on Jack. He mentioned that he was sick of spending his days fighting the worst of humanity and longed for the world to no longer need people like him.

Tess rubbed his back. She leaned over and softly said, "Maybe it's time to make a change. You've served your country for so long. No one would bat an eyelash."

He shrugged. "Thanks, sweetheart. We'll see. It was just a long week."

"Well, I have something that will lighten the mood," Omar said.

"Please, tell us," Jack said.

"Butterfly, shall I tell them about your treachery, or would you like to do the honors?"

Tess picked up a pretzel and lobbed it at him. "I don't know what you're making such a big deal about. I just did what had to be done."

Omar laughed. "I know, but the way you did it was bloody hysterical."

"What's he talking about?" Jack asked.

"Nothing, it was just a silly phone call," Tess replied.

"It was priceless," Omar said.

"This is gonna be good. Tell us," Bobby said.

Omar looked at Tess and she raised her eyebrows.

"It's all you," she said. "Honestly, there's nothing to even tell."

"Let them be the judge of that," Omar said, hurling a pretzel at her. "So, you all know that our Tess is literally the sweetest person in the world."

They all agreed. "Without a doubt."

She shook her head. "You're all ridiculous."

"Well, even though she's as kind as can be to everyone at least 99 percent of the time, every once in a blue moon, someone will tick her off and she'll cut them down in the most brilliant, most uniquely Tess way."

"I do not," Tess protested.

"Uh, yes you do. And because everyone always expects you to be so good-natured, it's hilarious when you get really worked up. Plus, you're smart as hell and quick on your feet, so you can come up with some real doozies," Omar said. "So today, she was at her friend Kate's, AKA she was at the White House with the president, making muffins or something."

"Scones. We made scones," Tess said indignantly.

Omar shook his head. "Yeah, I know. I just wanted to make you say it." She stuck her tongue out at him and he chuckled. "Anyway, Abdul and I are putting the finishing touches on his project and we ran into a little snag. The members of the executive committee are supposed to attend all the summits; it's part of the agreement. Well, this one guy, Bernard Bentley, an American with deep pockets from big oil, decided that he's willing to attend the Venice and Paris summits, but has a bit of a problem going to the Middle East. I forgot that Tess was hanging out with her new BFF, so I called to ask her advice on how best to handle it. She knows Bernard."

"Before this goes any further, let me just say that I have toured all over the Middle East and it was hardly as luxurious as the Dubai resort where these summits will take place. I went everywhere, meeting with women in secret, constantly under threat. These people will be sipping cocktails in a five-star hotel. Furthermore, and this is not directed at Omar because he didn't know where I was, let me just remind everyone that I don't like when my time with my friends is interrupted, especially not by an arrogant man like Bernard Bentley. Perhaps it made me a bit cross, and so I was, uh, quick with my words."

Omar burst into hysterics. When he regained his composure, he managed to say, "Uh, yes, perhaps. But honestly Butterfly, I thought it was bloody brilliant. You have a low threshold for BS, and you do know how to take care of things."

Tess flung another pretzel at him.

"Anyway, I called Tess and she put me on speakerphone because apparently her hands were covered in powdered sugar. Thankfully, she did tell me she was with the president before I could embarrass myself. I told them about the situation with Bernard, and the president offered to call him personally. Tess said, 'Madam President, if it's all right with you, I'd like to speak to Bernard. I can take care of this straight away.' The president agreed and Tess asked me to patch Bernard into the call. Bernard was sheepish from the outset, as the last thing he wants to do is make waves with president or with Tess. So, Tess said, 'Hello, Bernard,' and he tried to make friendly small talk. She shut him down immediately and said, 'Bernard, I hear that you're reluctant to go to Abu Dhabi or Dubai. Perhaps I should just book you a suite at the Four Seasons Hotel George V in Paris; then, I can draw you a bubble bath, pop open a bottle of rosé, and cut up your filet mignon. Would you be more comfortable with that?' Before he could respond, she snipped, 'Bernard, I don't have time for this. Grow a pair and get on that plane. Now I really must go, the president and I have to glaze our scones.'"

Everyone burst into laughter, practically falling out of their chairs.

Eventually, through fits of hysterics, Jack asked, "Did you really tell him to grow a pair?"

"Maybe," she replied, blushing.

"What did Bernard do?" Joe asked Omar.

"Oh, he'll be on that bloody plane. He asked me to apologize to Tess and the president for causing any strife."

Everyone continued laughing.

"You offered to cut his meat. I can't take it! You're such a badass," Bobby said, trying to catch his breath.

"The best part was when she said, 'The president and I have to glaze our scones.' It was so surreal and wickedly bizarre," Omar said.

"Tess, how did the president respond when you hung up?" Bobby asked.

"She just looked at me and said, 'Well done,' and we went back to preparing the glaze for our scones and resumed our conversation about the trade wars with China."

"Oh my God, I can hardly breathe," Jack said, taking a gulp of his drink.

"I told you," Omar said.

"I honestly don't see what's so funny," Tess protested.

"Sweetheart, it's just because of how sweet you are and how unusual the situation was."

"Plus, most people don't say 'grow a pair' to an oil tycoon in front of the president," Omar squealed, still laughing.

Tess smiled. "Kate didn't mind."

Soon, three months had passed. Tess wrote and regularly visited the president, with whom she'd quickly become good friends. Jack worked doggedly, though the toll it took increased. They spent time with their friends, and prioritized time alone together, falling more in love with each passing day.

CHAPTER 7

That Thursday morning, when Jack's alarm sounded, he brushed Tess's hair back and whispered, "Good morning, sweetheart."

She yawned and grumbled, "Good morning, my love."

"Come take a shower with me," Jack said.

"Oh baby, I can't today. I'm meeting Omar for our weekly breakfast. I have to review some documents he emailed, and I wanted to squeeze in a quick run on the treadmill first."

"There are better ways to burn off energy," Jack said, kissing her neck.

"Baby, if you keep that up, it will be impossible to resist."

"That's the idea."

She wormed away, picked up a pillow, and playfully tossed it at his head. "You'll have to wait until tonight, but I'll be thinking about how sexy you are all day."

He smiled. "Okay, you win, but it's going to be hard to concentrate today. If our national security suffers, it's on you."

She giggled. "Before I see Omar, I wanted to ask you something. The worldwide release of my new novel is in less than two months. I promised my publisher I'd do at least a few signings, and I know Omar's going to pester me about it. I was thinking maybe here in DC, plus New York and LA. You know I've kept my LA house because it's such a good investment, and you've never seen it."

"Sounds good. You know I'd go anywhere with you," he replied.

"Jack, ever since the gala, I've been thinking: you've never been to Japan, and it's such a special place. What do you think about taking a trip to Asia to promote some of the translations? We've never traveled abroad together. I was thinking maybe stops in China, Taiwan, Korea, and Japan. The readers in that part of the world have been especially generous. They were always some of my favorites to meet. It doesn't get too intense. They don't all tell me their stories of trauma; they just ask me to sign their books and take photos."

He smiled brightly and kissed the side of her head. "I would love that."

"Omar will be thrilled. It drives him nuts that I haven't done any international promotion in over three years."

"I know, I think he'll be stunned. Why now?" Jack asked.

"Because I'd be with you. I would love to show you Tokyo and Kyoto; they're magical. I can't even imagine what it will be like with you. You'll love Japan as much as I do."

"Sweetheart, I would love being anywhere with you."

"It will be different being there with you. I'll be able to pop in and out to do the Tess Lee book signing thing, and spend the rest of the time as Tess Miller, your personal tour guide."

"And my lover. My irresistible lover," he said.

She blushed. "You had better jump in the shower before you're late."

"Last chance," he said.

"Tonight, baby. I'm running up to the gym. Have a great day."

"You too, sweetheart."

***

When Tess arrived at the hotel restaurant, the maître d' greeted her warmly. "Ms. Lee, it's always a pleasure. We have your usual table. Your guest is waiting."

"Thank you, Alfred. How's your son doing? Did he get those grad school applications in?" she replied as he escorted her to the table.

"He's doing very well, thank you. He just sent them out the other day."

"That's wonderful. I hope he has lots of choices."

They arrived at the corner window table, but Omar was so preoccupied scrolling through messages on his phone that he didn't notice. He was startled when she leaned down to hug him.

"Oh, Butterfly. I'm sorry. With the upcoming release, all of your international publishers have been emailing incessantly."

"Funny you should mention that," she said, taking a seat. "I was thinking of doing a short book tour in Asia. Jack and I were just talking about it this morning. What do you say?"

"Holy hell, I'm speechless," he replied.

"Well, it's about time. I've been trying to shut you up for years!"

He laughed and raised his water glass. "Good one, Butterfly."

She smiled.

"But seriously, why the change of heart?"

They were interrupted by the waitress, who approached with a sterling silver coffee pot. "Good morning, Ms. Lee. I have the French roast you like," she said as she poured the coffee.

"Good morning, Bridget. It's nice to see you," Tess said.

"Would you both like the usual or should I give you a minute?"

"My usual please," Tess replied.

"Today, I think I'll branch out and try the spinach omelet," Omar said.

As soon as the waitress was out of earshot, Omar said, "Don't you find it strange that we could go anywhere for brunch, but we come to the same hotel every week? Who eats breakfast at a hotel in a city in which they live?"

"It's the only place that will make me two plain poached eggs without giving me a hard time about it. Besides, there's something about hotels. There's a certain peacefulness I can't quite explain. I find it reassuring. Maybe it's a force of habit from being on the road for so many years."

"While we're on the subject, are you serious about Asia?"

She nodded. "Jack's never been. It will be a different experience to go with him. Everything is different with him. But let's keep the schedule light please, just a few book signings so I can spend the rest of the time sightseeing. I want to see everything anew, through his eyes. I can't wait to show him Japan. He'll love the pagodas and shrines at Ueno Park. All I want to do is stroll through the park, holding his hand and breathing the air."

"He's going to need to take at least a couple of weeks off work. You really should think about what I said to you before. You and Jack can build any life you choose. He doesn't need to be chained to a desk, nor you to DC."

"I know. I've been thinking about it since we got back from Hawaii. It's just, it's just…"

"Have you mentioned it to Jack?"

She shook her head and her gaze fell downward.

Omar placed his hand on hers. She looked up at him, her eyes wet. "He loves you, Butterfly, with all his heart. He always will."

She smiled and wiped the corners of her eyes. "Now, what about you and Clay? I know you've been working on things. Last week at the bar when he and I were dancing, he told me he's never been happier, and he had his arm around you all night. It would seem that things are better."

Omar grinned from ear to ear. "I was waiting to tell you in person. He proposed. We're getting married!"

"Oh my goodness!" she exclaimed, jumping up. She threw her arms around him and they bounced up and down like children. "Omar, I'm so happy for you both I could burst! It's fantastic beyond words." They hugged for an eternity before they plunked back down, each smiling brightly. "When did this happen? Tell me everything. I guess this means there's no more doubt."

He shook his head. "Nothing ever happened between him and that man. I'm certain. It was just my insecurity getting the best of me. Maybe it's a human thing, to doubt, to doubt that we are worthy, to doubt that we are truly loved. But Butterfly, we do deserve love and we are enough. I know that's how you always feel when you're with Jack. Try to remember that in the moments when you're not together."

She became misty, smiling through her watery eyes. "Thank you," she whispered. "Now, tell me every last detail. This positively must be celebrated."

***

Jack was reviewing a file with Bobby when the mail runner knocked on his door.

"Come in," Jack called.

"Sorry to bother you, but this envelope arrived addressed to your attention, and it's marked urgent," he said, handing Jack a large envelope with no return address or postage.

Jack opened the envelope and the color drained from his face. He sprang from his seat. "Where did this come from?" he loudly demanded.

"I don't know, sir. It was on the mail table."

"What is it?" Bobby asked.

Jack handed him the paper, which read: *Your wife belongs with me. I would rather see her dead than with you. Let her go or I'll kill her and make you watch. Then I'll kill you. Slowly.*

"Oh my God," Bobby mumbled.

Jack grabbed his phone and called Tess. It rang several times before she answered.

"Hi, honey. I just walked in the door. You won't believe it – Omar and Clay are engaged."

"Sweetheart, I need to talk to you."

"Hang on a second, I'm opening something. There was an envelope at the front door. It's so strange, there's nothing on it except for my name."

"Tess, put me on speakerphone and tell me what's in it."

Tess gasped.

"Sweetheart, what is it?"

"Uh, I'm not sure. It's some kind of threat. There's a letter and photographs."

"What does it say?"

"It is time you know the truth about your husband. He's a violent man and a liar. You cannot stay with him. You belong with me. I'm going to save you. I'll be in touch." She paused and softly said, "And there are photographs, Jack."

"What are they?"

"I don't know. Bodies. Dead people. A few look like they're from some kind of combat situation, others look like a crime scene. Then there are pictures of you in a room, holding a man against a wall, bending someone's arm, up in someone's face. Who would send this?"

"Tess, where are you in the house? I have a gun stashed on every floor."

"The kitchen. I just got home. But Jack…"

"Turn on the security alarm right now and get the gun from the safe in the coat closet. Sit in the living room and wait for me. I'm on my way."

"I'm turning the alarm on, but Jack, I don't want to get the gun. You know I could never use that thing. I'm more likely to hurt myself by mistake."

"Sweetheart, just do this for me, please. Do it now. I'm on my way. Don't open the door for anyone, not even someone you know. And don't hang up the phone. I'm going to put you on hold until I get in the car."

"Jack," she said softly.

"Just do it. Please."

"Okay."

Jack looked at Bobby. "Put Joe in charge of the office and send the letter for analysis. Call Metro PD and send them and a team of agents to my house. I'll meet them there," he yelled, racing out the door.

CHAPTER 8

When Jack got to the house, he turned off the alarm and flew inside. Tess was sitting on the couch in the living room, the gun and contents of the envelope strewn on the coffee table. She leapt up and they embraced. He rubbed the back of her head. "It's okay, baby. Everything is going to be okay."

"I know," she said, holding him tightly.

A moment passed and she sat down. He knelt on the floor in front of her. "Are you all right?"

"I'm fine, really."

He picked up the letter and flipped through the photographs, careful to only touch the edges. He looked down and shook his head. "I'm so sorry, Tess."

"You haven't done anything to be sorry for."

His head was still hung. "I never wanted you to see these things. I never wanted you to see me this way."

She touched his chin and lifted his head. "Jack, you told me about all of this the first weekend we spent together. There's nothing new here. I see the man I love doing an exceedingly difficult job and pictures that are taken out of context."

"Hearing about it and seeing it isn't the same."

"I'm a writer. I have a pretty vivid imagination."

He smiled faintly.

"You told me about doing things far worse than what's shown in these photographs."

"Yeah," he muttered. "Foolishly, I had hoped I could tell you those things and then you'd never think about them again."

"I haven't. I love you."

He gently pressed his lips to hers. "I love you so much, Tess. I'm going to fix this."

There was a pounding on the front door. "Stay here," Jack said.

He returned a moment later with Bobby and half a dozen federal agents.

"Do a full sweep of the house," Bobby ordered the others, who fanned out in all directions. "Hey, Tess. Don't worry. We're going to keep you safe."

She smiled. "I'm not worried. I just don't understand why someone doesn't want me to be with Jack."

"We'll figure it out," Bobby said. "Jack, do you have any video surveillance on the house?"

"No. I had to convince Tess just to get a basic alarm system. She didn't want one with video."

"I was just trying to protect our privacy. I was worried about video getting stolen and ending up on one of those gossip shows. I'm sorry. I didn't know..." Tess said.

"It's fine," Jack said. He handed Bobby the contents of the envelope. "Get this processed."

Bobby read the note and flipped through the photographs. "When were these taken?"

"The first few are from a mission in the Gulf. Things went badly. There were civilian casualties, women and children. That one's from a takedown we did about five years ago, all confirmed terrorists. The others are stills taken from video surveillance of interrogations I conducted, several years ago. They were all extreme situations with imminent threats we were trying to prevent. Bobby, whoever did this has access to Bureau files."

"Yeah, I know. We'll find out who could have gotten these and how. Are you thinking that this is somebody who has a grudge against you? Someone from an old case?" Bobby asked.

"Yes," Jack said emphatically, before quickly backtracking. "I don't know. Maybe."

"Both letters said something about Tess belonging with him. We can't rule out that this is some kind of stalker or someone from her past," Bobby said. "Tess, can you think of anyone we should look into?"

"No."

"Tess, think hard," Jack said softly.

"Well, I do have some intense fans." She got quiet for a moment and then said, "Also, I get hate mail from time to time."

"We need to review everything," Bobby said.

"I never see any of it personally. It goes to my assistant, Crystal. If there's something of concern, she passes it on to Omar. They shield me from it."

"Please get in touch with them. Tell them to give us access to everything we need," Bobby said. "I'll follow up."

"I guess I'll have to tell Omar what's going on. I hate to upset him."

Jack knelt down and took her hands. "He can handle it. I'll call him while you get in touch with Crystal."

"The letter says he's going to contact Tess," Bobby said. "We don't know how that will happen, so let's keep her cell and the landline free in case he calls. I'll make sure we're set up to do a trace."

"Okay," Jack said.

The agents returned to the main floor and informed Bobby that the house was clear. Bobby ordered two to the front door, two to the back door, and told the others to get ready to run a trace and start processing data. Still holding the letter and pictures, he turned to Jack, "I'll get going with these and give you two a minute."

Jack rubbed Tess's hands. "Sweetheart, I promise you, I will take care of this."

"I'm really fine. I'm mostly just concerned about you."

He let out a huff. "Of course you are."

"I mean it, Jack." She interlaced her fingers with his. "I can see the worry in your eyes."

"This is my worst fear. It's the reason I didn't allow myself to be in a relationship for all those years when I was working in the field. I never wanted to endanger the people in my life. When we met, I already had a desk job and thought it would be safe. I never wanted anything I've done to cause you any harm. I'm so sorry."

"Please stop saying you're sorry. This isn't your fault. We'll get through it. The whole thing could be a hoax, too. Do you want to know my only regret?"

"What?"

"That I didn't get in the shower with you this morning. It would have been a much better day."

He laughed and looked a little lighter. "I have to go help them," he said.

She nodded. "But first, kiss me like you mean it."

He leaned in and kissed her fervently. "I always mean it."

***

When Omar arrived an hour later, Tess was in the kitchen making a cup of jasmine tea. He was holding a large cardboard box, which he placed on the bar. "Hello, Butterfly," he said, giving her a peck on the cheek. "I know you're a writer, but bloody hell, must you always be so dramatic?"

She laughed. "I'll do whatever it takes to see you twice in one day."

"Glad you haven't lost your sense of humor. Seriously, how are you holding up?"

"I'm fine. As you can see, it's like an episode of some crime procedural show in here," she said, gesturing to the agents and police officers meandering around. "Perhaps I'll get an idea for a book. I've never written a thriller."

"That's the spirit," he replied.

She dunked her teabag into the mug. "Hey, come here," Omar said. He hugged her tightly. "Everything will be okay."

"I know. Did you know the letter said I don't belong with Jack?" she whispered.

"No one is going to come between you and Jack, Butterfly."

Jack and Bobby bounded into the room.

"Ah, and here he is now," Omar said.

"Hi, Omar. I hear congratulations are in order," Jack said.

Omar smiled. "I know this isn't the time."

"Yeah. Thank you for coming so quickly."

"Of course. Crystal has forwarded your men all the emails we've flagged over the past year, but she can go back further if you need. Being a bit paranoid myself, I've always saved the strange pieces of snail mail from her self-proclaimed number one fans and the like. They're all in there," Omar said, pointing to the box.

"Thank you. We'll start going through it," Bobby said, picking it up.

"Honestly, you're probably wasting your time," Tess said. "I've always envisioned them as enthusiastic readers."

"Butterfly, some of them are creepy at best, others are downright depraved."

"Nonsense," she rebuffed.

"You say tomato, I say psychopath," Omar retorted.

She rolled her eyes and turned her attention to Jack. "Any news?"

Jack shook his head. "There weren't any fingerprints or trace DNA on anything that was sent, and the paper and ink were generic. We're trying to find a trail from the photographs, but nothing yet. I'm going to start combing through back cases to identify people that may have it out for me, a list which is sure to be long." Jack's phone rang. He looked at the screen and said, "It's coming from the White House. I need to take this," and then excused himself.

"Butterfly, I'm going to pour myself a cup of tea. I'm staying here with you until this nightmare is over."

"You're so sweet, but..."

"Don't even try it. I'm here, however long it takes."

She smiled and gave him another hug. "Thank you."

They took their tea and sat in the living room, Tess clutching her cell phone. "They think he might call me, whoever this is. They're hoping to trace the call."

"I can't believe you may have to talk to this lunatic."

She squeezed her eyelids shut and shook her head. "Everything will be all right."

Jack walked into the room.

"That was the president on the phone. She heard about what's going on here and wanted to remind me that you're a national treasure and says I should use every available resource to protect you."

"Well, that's very sweet, but it seems ridiculous," Tess quipped.

"No, it isn't," he said, leaning down and kissing the top of her head. "She also reminded me that you're a dear friend. She said she doesn't want to intrude while there's so much going on, but insisted that you can call her anytime." He turned to Omar. "Can I please speak to you for a minute?"

Jack and Omar walked to the far corner of the kitchen. Jack used his hands to motion that they should speak quietly.

"How is Tess doing?" he asked.

"Honestly, she seems fine. You, on the other hand, don't look so good."

"Don't worry about me. Why didn't you tell me about the hate mail she gets?"

"She's famous, Jack. Surely you must realize she gets her fair share of strange mail. This has gone on for over fifteen years. There's never been any problem. I'm sorry. I didn't think…"

"I'm sorry. It's okay," Jack said.

"There is one thing I should tell you, but I didn't think I should say anything in front of Tess."

"What?"

"When you two got married, there were some super fans who were upset."

"Like stalkers who have a thing for her?" Jack asked.

Omar shook his head. "No, her books are a lifeline to many of her readers, they're sacred to them. Some were concerned that if Tess had a happy life, she'd no longer be able to write the same way. She writes about pain, loss, loneliness, heartache. I think a lot of fans wondered if she'd still be able to tap into their pain."

"People are so messed up," Jack said.

"Tess doesn't know anything about this. You know how protective she feels about your relationship. I never saw any reason to upset her."

"Okay," Jack said.

Tess's phone rang. "Jack, I'm getting a call from a blocked number," she hollered. She sprinted into the kitchen and placed the phone on the bar.

"Bobby," Jack screamed. He turned to Tess. "Put it on speakerphone. The idea is to keep the person on the phone for as long as possible. The more he talks, the greater likelihood he will trip up and say something that helps us identify him. I'll tell you when to pick up."

Bobby gave the green light.

"Answer it," Jack said.

"Hello?" she said.

It was an automated message from her wireless provider. She hung up. Ten minutes later, Tess's phone rang again. It was another blocked caller. She sat on a barstool with Jack on the stool beside her. Bobby gave her the go-ahead and she answered the phone, clicking speaker.

"Hello?"

An electronically altered voice responded, "Did you get the pictures I sent? With the feds and cops swarming your house, I assume you did."

She looked at Jack and he nodded for her to talk. Then, he gestured for the agents to canvass the area.

"Who is this?" she asked.

"Someone who cares about you. Did you get the pictures?"

"Yes. I don't understand why you sent those to me. What do you want?"

"I want to show you the truth about your husband."

"He's told me about everything in those photographs. He was just doing his job."

"He's lying to you. Don't listen to him."

"Why are you doing this to us?"

"I'm protecting you from a mistake you made."

"Who are you? Do I know you?" she asked.

"The more prudent question is: Do you know who you married?"

"Yes, I do. What I don't know is why you're harassing us. Please, stop this before it goes too far."

"I know the feds are trying to trace this call, but they're wasting their time. You need to listen to me."

"I am listening," Tess said.

"I'll be in touch again soon."

"Wait," she said, but he had already hung up.

Jack reached over and embraced her.

"I'm sorry, I tried to keep him on the line," she whispered.

"You did great, baby," Jack said, rubbing her back.

"Jack, he's watching the house," she whispered.

"I know, baby. Don't worry. We'll find him."

"Please don't let go," she said.

"I'm right here," he said, holding her tightly.

A few moments passed and Jack leaned back. He held Tess's hand and looked up as Bobby and another agent returned from outside.

"There's no sign of him. This guy knows what he's doing. It was a burner phone, impossible to trace," Bobby said.

"Damn it," Jack muttered.

"But we did record the call so we can play it back and see if anything pops out," Bobby said.

"Sweetheart, I have to go help them. I need you to hang out with Omar for a while," Jack said.

"Don't worry, we'll have oodles of fun. Perhaps we can watch *Psycho* or one of those gruesome *Halloween* movies with the serial killers," Omar joked.

Tess giggled. "You're terrible."

***

Three hours later, Tess and Omar were halfway through their second slasher film when an agent came upstairs, holding an envelope.

Jack and Bobby were sitting in the kitchen, data mining. The agent handed the envelope to Jack. "We just noticed this on the windshield of your car. It has your name on it."

"Are you fucking kidding me? The car is parked in front of the damn house! How the hell did he leave something there without any of us seeing him?"

"The agents are stationed at the front and back door, but the car isn't in our sightline. He must have slipped by quickly or had a courier drop it."

Jack put on a pair of gloves and opened the envelope. He pulled out a letter and a bullet, then handed them to Bobby, walked over to the wall, and punched a hole in it. "Fuck!" he screamed.

Tess rushed over. "Baby, what is it?"

"Please, just go sit with Omar," he replied.

"No, not with you so upset," she said, rubbing his back. "What is it?"

"It's just an empty threat. There's no reason to worry you more."

"The only person I'm worried about is you." She turned to Bobby. "Please show it to me."

He showed her the letter, which read: *She's mine. Let her go or I'll kill her.*

Tess turned back toward Jack. He was clutching his head in his hands. "Honey, it's all right. He's just a creep. For all we know, these are just idle threats and we're all overreacting."

"Jack, do you want to pull your car into the garage?" Bobby asked.

"No. Leave it where it is and station an undercover officer to watch it. Maybe he'll try it again and we can grab him," Jack said, his chest heaving.

"Baby, please try to relax," Tess said.

"I'm fine, just go sit with Omar."

"Jack, you're clearly not fine."

"Just go sit with Omar," he snapped, a little too forcefully. He caught himself and softened his tone. "Please, baby."

"Come on, Butterfly, let's finish watching our movie," Omar said.

Tess rejoined Omar in the living room. She gestured for him to sit next to her on the couch. "Jack isn't doing well. I've never seen him like this," she whispered.

"This is a high-stress situation. He's worried about you."

"Yeah, well, I'm worried about him."

***

Tess and Omar watched movies for hours, but Tess kept one eye on Jack, who was stomping back and forth, muttering things, and yelling at the other agents. For a while, he sat at the bar in the kitchen, poring over old case files for criminals he had busted who might be seeking revenge, calling out for Bobby to check on this one or that one. Tess watched as he became increasingly agitated, hunched over the laptop, a scowl etched on his face. She walked over and ran her fingers through his hair. "Not now, Tess. I have to get through this," he said.

"I'm just concerned about you."

"I'm fine," he insisted.

At eight o'clock, Omar had pizza and salads delivered for the whole team. He, Tess, and Bobby sat at the kitchen bar together, but Tess barely picked at her salad. Omar tried to encourage her to eat, but it was in vain. Jack walked in after meeting with a couple of agents downstairs.

"Honey, sit down and have a bite," Tess begged.

"I'm fine."

"Jack, everybody has to eat, even you. Please, just have a slice of pizza and something to drink before you get dehydrated or you'll be no use to anyone."

Bobby pulled out a stool. "Come on man, you need to eat."

"I said I'm fine."

Tess was about to say something when her phone rang. It was a blocked number. Jack barreled over and stood beside her. Bobby set up the trace and gave her the signal to answer.

"Hello?"

"Please don't be afraid of me," the altered voice said.

"You're sending me death threats."

"I don't want to do that. I have no choice."

"Yes, you do. You can stop all of this now."

"How could you let him talk his way out of the photographs I sent? The way he abuses people, the way he abuses his power. I will make you see what kind of man you married. He's a violent liar. I'll be in touch tomorrow. Get your beauty sleep."

"Wait," she called, but he had already hung up. "I'm sorry, I tried."

"It's okay, baby," Jack replied, rubbing her shoulders.

"There was something about that call," she muttered.

"What?" he asked.

"Did you recognize something?" Bobby asked.

"Yes. When he said, 'Get your beauty sleep,' there was something familiar about it, but I can't place it."

"Think, Tess!" Jack bellowed.

She looked up at him, her eyes wide. "I'm trying. I'm sorry. I…"

"It's okay, sweetheart. I'm sorry I yelled. I know you're trying."

"Please Jack, just eat a little something and drink a glass of water. Please."

He sat down and they ate in silence.

When they were done with their meal, Tess said, "I'm going to try to get some sleep. Just wake me if I'm needed."

"Okay," Jack said.

"Tess, I'm going to crash in one of your guest rooms, if that's all right," Bobby said.

"Well, of course you're always welcome, but we don't want to interrupt your life. You should go home and be with Gina," she replied.

"No way. I'm here for the duration. Gina will understand. We have a night crew coming to swap places with our agents soon. The house is covered."

"And of course I'll be here, Butterfly, so if you want to snuggle and watch movies, you know where to find me," Omar said.

Tess smiled. "Thank you both." She walked over to Jack and embraced him, savoring the strength of his arms. "I'm fine, really," she said. "Please try not to worry so much."

***

When Tess awoke a little after midnight, Jack's side of the bed was empty. She stumbled into the kitchen and found Omar, Jack, and Bobby all sitting at the bar. Jack was replaying the two recorded phone calls.

"Honey, it's after midnight. Please come to bed," Tess said.

"Tess is right," Bobby said. "We've listened to that thing thirty times."

"We don't have any other leads," Jack protested.

"There are guys at the office working on this, our best guys, and people outside making sure we're secure. Get some sleep so you'll be in better shape tomorrow. We need you clear headed," Bobby urged.

A scowl on his face, Jack ignored them and hit play again. When the recording ended, he muttered, "When we find this motherfucker, I'm going to tear him apart with my bare hands. I'm going to gut him. They'll need a dozen bags for all his body parts. He fucked with the wrong guy."

Tess walked over to him, put her hand on his back, and said, "Honey, please try to calm down. I really think you need some rest."

"Damn it, Tess, I said no!" he screamed.

She stepped back in shock. She stood for a moment and then turned to walk back to her bedroom. Omar grabbed her hand. "Butterfly," he said.

"It's fine," she replied softly.

When she was out of the room, Bobby said, "Jack, you've got to pull it together, man. If you keep this up, the only person Tess is going to fear is you. You're losing it. All you're doing is showing her that this asshole is right and that you're violent and dangerous. There's nothing we can do right now. I'm going to crash for a few hours, and I think you should do the same." On his way out of the room, he turned to Omar and said, "You should get some sleep, too."

"I'll be up soon," Omar replied.

Jack stood up, paced in a circle, and punched another hole in the wall. "Fuck!" he screeched.

"You feel better?" Omar asked.

"Just go to bed," Jack said.

"Jack, I've stayed up because I'm concerned about you. You're becoming totally unhinged. I've never seen you speak to Tess that way, and especially with what she's going through. I know you think all of this is your fault, but it isn't."

"Yes, it is," he moaned, gripping his head.

"No, it isn't. You must accept that. And you need to talk to Tess. Tell her how you feel, tell her what you're scared of. If you don't, it will destroy you and this asshole will win."

"I don't want to frighten her," Jack replied.

"The only thing she's frightened of is what's happening to you. Jack please, I'm your friend and I love Tess more than anything in this world. If I thought you staying up all night to beat yourself up was going to help, I wouldn't say a word. Go talk with her. Then, try to get some sleep so you're in a better frame of mind tomorrow, and hopefully we'll catch this lunatic."

Jack nodded.

When he walked into their bedroom, Tess was sitting up in bed, the small lamp on her nightstand glowing dimly on her face.

"I'm so sorry, sweetheart."

"You don't have to be," she said. She turned down the blankets on his side of the bed. "Please come here."

He took his shoes off and climbed into bed.

She kissed him softly. "Baby, talk to me."

"When we fell in love, I didn't even want to say the words to express how I felt about you without also telling you everything I've done. And I was terrified you wouldn't be able to love me in return if you knew."

"But I loved you then and I love you now, more than anything."

"It's a terrible thing, taking someone's life." Jack paused and ran his hand through his hair. "The collateral damage that you can't stop, innocent people getting hurt. Killing, hurting, or threatening people; it's awful. You just block everything else out so you can do what must be done for the job you signed up for. That doesn't mean it's easy or that it's how you wish things were. Some days, I'm horrified by what I've been able to do, no matter the reason. Now this monster is taking all the worst things I think about myself, the things I've struggled to come to terms with, and he's using them to hurt the person I love the most."

She brushed her fingers along his face.

He started to cry. "Nothing in this world is more important to me than you are. I would do anything for you. These are my worst fears, all of them. I never wanted the things I've done to cause you pain or put you in harm's way."

"What's happening isn't your fault. Love isn't only good things. There's always pain attached, like a shadow."

He looked at her with tears in his eyes. "You've always said I make you feel safe, and now, now I feel like I can't protect you."

"Baby, when I say that you make me feel safe, it has nothing to do with your job or your physical strength. It's because of the way you love me. When you look at me, I know you see exactly who I am and I see exactly who you are. That's what makes me feel safe. I feel safe being with someone so good who loves me so well. You make me feel safe to be myself."

"When Gracie was sick, I was completely powerless. It was agony. There's no way to describe the anguish of watching your child die. I didn't think anything could ever hurt that much. Then, when your father died and you relived all that childhood abuse and I watched you suffer, I felt it all over again, completely useless." He stopped to wipe his eyes and take a steadying breath. "This should be something I can deal with. I'm angry at myself. I'm failing you."

"You are the strongest, most wonderful, generous, loving man. You could never fail me. Just be you. Don't let this turn you into something else. Don't become what you fear."

He looked at her and cradled her face in his hands. "God, I love you." He pulled her close, rubbed the tip of his nose to hers, and kissed her passionately. "I can't lose you, Tess. Do you understand? I can't lose you."

"I know you're scared, but please believe me when I say that I'm not. We're going to get through this. The important thing is that we're together and we love each other. The rest isn't in our control any more than the things that have happened to our friends and to other people every day. This just happens to be a little more unusual."

He smiled through his tears.

"Jack, it's not about what happens, but how we deal with it. I know deep in my heart it will all work out. But you need to lean on me, baby."

"I love you so much, Tess."

"I love you, too. Let's try to get some sleep." She reached over and switched off the lamp. They lay down together and she draped her arm over him. "Thank you for talking to me."

CHAPTER 9

Jack and Tess strolled into the kitchen just after seven o'clock. Omar and Bobby were chatting and eating bagels.

"Good morning, guys," Bobby said.

"Good morning, Butterfly," Omar said, kissing Tess's forehead. "Hope you don't mind, we helped ourselves. There's plenty of coffee."

"Thanks," Jack said. He turned to Bobby, "Any update?"

Bobby shook his head.

"Sweetheart, do you want me to make you some oatmeal?"

"Thanks, baby," she replied, taking a seat on the stool next to Omar.

"So, what's on the agenda today, Butterfly? I'm thinking that we should watch a marathon of those Lifetime 'women-in-peril' movies they love so much – you know, a cheerleader murdered by her coach or a hooker trying to escape her pimp."

She knuckled the top of his head.

"That's okay, I'll even suffer with bad hair today for you, considering that you've got a stalker trying to kill you and all."

She laughed.

They ate breakfast, almost as if it were a normal morning, until it was time for the shift change among the federal agents guarding the house, reminding them it was not.

"Omar, let's do some work, since we're stuck here," Tess said. "We can watch cheesy movies later."

Around ten o'clock, Tess and Omar were reviewing licensing deals when her phone rang. It was him. When the agent signaled, Jack nodded for her to answer.

"Hello?" she said.

"Good morning, Tess. How are you feeling?" he asked.

"I'm distressed. Please stop this."

"Have you had time to think about what I've said?"

"About you threatening my life? Yes, it's hard to think about anything else."

"I'm sorry that I've scared you. I would never want to hurt you. I only want to get you away from your husband."

"Why? What has he ever done to you?"

"You don't belong with him. You belong with me. I'm going to take care of you."

"Who is this?"

"You'll find out soon enough."

"Please, why are you doing this?" she pleaded.

"Because you married the wrong man," he said, and then the line went dead.

"We couldn't trace it," an agent reported.

"You did great, sweetheart," Jack said.

"Oh my God. I know who it is," Tess mumbled, her head hung.

Jack put his hand on her shoulder.

"It's Ray Potter," she said softly.

"Oh my God," Omar muttered.

"Who's Ray Potter?" Jack asked.

She looked up at him, deep sadness in her eyes. "We grew up together. He was my high school boyfriend. He asked me to marry him when we graduated, but I turned him down."

"Are you sure it's him?" Jack asked.

She nodded. "That's why he said I married the wrong man. I couldn't place it last night, but sometimes when he would drop me off at my house and we were trying to make my curfew, I would tell him that I didn't care if I was late. He would say, 'It's okay, you need your beauty sleep.' Jack, it's him. I'm certain."

Jack turned to Bobby and the other agent. "Start digging up everything you can on this guy." He turned his attention back to Tess. "When was the last time you saw him?"

"Over twenty years ago. I haven't seen him since I left home."

"Sweetheart, did he ever hit you or give you any reason to be afraid of him?"

She shook her head. "Nothing like that. He was good to me. He was always a little jealous, although he had no reason to be. He didn't like it when other guys talked to me or even looked at me for too long.

Sometimes, he'd get bent out of shape over nothing. I guess he was a little possessive, but we were young and it seemed normal at the time."

"Why did you turn down his proposal?"

"Because I didn't love him, not in that way."

"How'd he take it?"

"He said mean things, trying to hurt me. I felt badly for him; I knew he had imagined a whole life for us that was far from the life I imagined for myself. He didn't know about my family and why I needed to get out of there."

"Is there anything you can tell us about his life since high school?"

"After graduation, he joined the Marines. That's all I know. I don't keep in touch with anyone from that time in my life."

"Don't worry, we'll find him."

Her eyes started to tear. "Jack, I can't believe he would do this to me."

He wrapped his arms around her and rubbed her back. She rested her head on his shoulder. "I'm so sorry, sweetheart."

After a few moments, Tess pulled away. Jack used his thumbs to gently wipe the tears that had trickled down her face. "I promise everything will be okay," he said.

"If you guys don't need me, I'd like to go lie down for a little while. I just want to be alone," she said.

"Of course. We'll come get you if we need you," he replied.

Omar looked at her earnestly. "Butterfly, are you okay?"

"No," she said softly, and she walked out of the room.

As soon as Tess was out of earshot, Omar said, "Jack, this isn't good. It may be too much for her."

"I know. I'm worried. This is the first time I can see this whole ordeal really affecting her."

"You know, the thing that's upset her the most so far is not the threat against her life, but that someone in the world doesn't want the two of you to be together. I'm sure you remember how she responded when her father died; that thought is unbearable to her. I'm amazed she's kept it together so well, which is a testament to the strength of the bond you two have built. But now, with this…"

"What's the deal with this guy, Ray?"

"He's the first person she had consensual sex with, which is not a small thing when your earlier experiences are violent. She trusted him."

Jack looked down.

"But it's more than that," Omar continued. "Over the years, as you know, many men have fallen for Tess."

"She's easy to love."

"Well, that's the thing: she doesn't think so. She would date men for very brief periods of time, and they were always far more interested in her than she was in them. Along the way, she racked up some impressive proposals. They weren't losers, far from it. Among others, one of Forbes' wealthiest businessmen and a rock star, but she'll be cross with me if I name names."

Jack smiled.

"She never really cared about any of them, but she would always tell me that they didn't really love her either, even though I think sometimes they absolutely did. She's told me she's only ever really believed that two men have loved her, only one of whom she loved in return."

"Ray. He was the other guy who loved her."

Omar nodded. "Jack, you have to understand that it's not a small thing for Tess. There's a deep part of her that feels unworthy of love, even now. It's not hard to understand when you consider how traumatic her childhood was. She believed her family loved her and look at what they did to her. Because of you, I think that 99 percent of her knows she deserves to be loved, but there is still that nagging 1 percent. This doesn't help."

"What do you think I should do?"

"Just be aware. The resilience we saw yesterday may vanish now that we know it's Ray. She may try to hide it for your sake. She knows the toll this is taking on you and she cares more about your well-being than she does her own. Just be as gentle as possible."

Jack nodded. "Thank you."

"I know you need to get back to work. I'll stay here in case Tess comes out. And Jack, even though this guy is the enemy to you now, don't be surprised if it's more complicated than that for Tess. If it is, that's not her fault. Remember when that dirt bag Arlo confronted her outside of Shelby's and you wanted to kill him?"

"Yes," Jack said.

"Tess said she loved you more than she hated him. That's what you need to do now. You need to love Tess more than you hate Ray. That's what she needs."

"Yeah, okay," Jack mumbled.

***

An hour later, Jack returned to the kitchen. Omar was sitting on a stool, drinking a cup of coffee.

"I made a fresh pot if you need some caffeine. Any news?" Omar asked.

"After the Marines, Ray joined the CIA. It explains how he was able to get those photographs, and why he's so good at covertly delivering these messages and covering his tracks. Two months ago, he disappeared, completely off the grid. No one he works with knows what happened to him. His mother lives in an assisted care facility in Arizona, but she suffers from dementia. He has a sister in Rhode Island and an ex-wife here in DC. We've tracked them both down and they're being questioned."

"Wow," Omar muttered. "So, Tess was right?"

"He's the guy," Jack replied.

"I know it's a good thing that we found out who's doing this, but for Tess's sake, I was hoping she was mistaken."

"Is she still in our room?" Jack asked.

Omar nodded.

"I'm going to check on her."

"Jack, please remember what I said. This hurts her and it's probably very confusing."

Jack nodded.

He opened the bedroom door to find Tess lying in bed, wide awake. She sprang up. "Do you need me?"

"No, sweetheart. I just came to spend some time with you."

"Oh," she said, and she plopped back down onto her side.

Jack sat on the edge of the bed, took his shoes off, and crawled in behind her. He put his arm across her waist.

"Is it him?" she whispered.

"Yes. He was in the CIA. That's how he's been able to do this. We have agents questioning his ex-wife and his sister. We'll find him."

"God, his sister Lucy was always so sweet. I can't believe she would know anything about this."

"He may have contacted her, that's all. It doesn't mean she knows what he's doing or is implicated in any way. Don't worry about any of it. It's being taken care of."

She rubbed his hand.

"Tess, I'm so sorry. I know this is awful for you. I'm here. I love you with my whole heart and we'll get through this."

"He's not a terrible person. I know what he's doing is horrible, but there must be a reason. He was good to me, Jack. I can't believe that he would ever really want to hurt me."

"Maybe something happened to him. His line of work isn't for everyone. It messes some people up," Jack replied.

"The things you said yesterday, about what you wanted to do when you found who was responsible. Jack, you can't hurt him. Promise me."

"Tess…"

"Jack please, promise me. I couldn't bear it."

"Okay, baby. If I can keep you safe without hurting him, I promise I will."

"Thank you. You know, he's in my debut novel. It's just a small part, but the protagonist talks about the first boy who loved her, and how guilty she feels that she didn't love him back because she wanted to, but she just didn't."

"You can't help who you love. It's not your fault."

She turned to face him and traced his jawline with her finger. "You're the only man I've ever truly loved. You're my one and only, forever."

He kissed her softly. "You're my everything, Tess. I promise you that this nightmare will be over soon."

"Can we just stay here like this for a little while longer?"

"As long as you want. They'll get us if we're needed. Shut your eyes, sweetheart. Let's get some rest."

***

Two hours later, Tess and Jack walked hand in hand into the kitchen. Omar, Bobby, and another agent were huddled together.

"What's the update?" Jack asked.

"Maybe Tess wants to come hang out with me and you guys can speak privately," Omar suggested.

"I want to hear what's going on," Tess said.

"Sweetheart, maybe it's better if…"

She interrupted. "I want to know. I'm sure you all mean well, but I'm not going to have a house full of men tell me what to do or keep things from me like I'm incompetent or a child. This is about me and I deserve to know. Please, Jack."

He nodded reluctantly.

She turned to Bobby, "Please tell us what's going on."

"His sister told us that Ray joined the Marines because he wanted to do something to make you proud of him. He tried to go home for holidays and during the summer whenever he could in the hopes of seeing you."

"When I left home, I never went back," Tess said.

Bobby nodded. "So, he told his sister he was going to track you down when you graduated college. He thought you had to get something out of your system but surely you would reconsider his proposal. He actually went to one of your book signings for your first novel, but when he saw the crowd and how famous you'd become, he left. His sister said he decided you were out of his league in that moment. She thought that was the end of it. He got married shortly after, but it only lasted two years. His ex-wife claims it was because he was still in love with 'some girl from high school,' so she left him."

"I don't understand why he's doing this now, after all these years," Tess said.

"There was a photograph of you and Jack in *The Post* after that gala a few months ago. A guy he worked with said that he showed him the newspaper and bragged that you were his first girlfriend. He said that he'd always assumed you must have married a millionaire, but it turned out you ended up with a guy like him. A few weeks later, he disappeared."

"Any leads on his whereabouts?" Jack asked.

Bobby shook his head. "He's been dark for two months, but since we've been interviewing people in his life I think it's safe to assume that he knows we've identified him."

"Well, if he calls back, I can try to talk to him. Maybe I can reach him," Tess said.

"We were thinking the same thing," Bobby replied. "And we're still doing everything we can to locate him and put an end to this."

Jack looked at Tess. "How are you doing?"

"I don't know," she said softly.

He hugged her.

"Well, despite how poorly my last suggestion was received, I'm going to make another one," Omar said.

"I'm glad to see you haven't lost your spirit," Tess quipped.

Omar smiled. "Butterfly, some food would do us all good. Let's get something delivered and we can sit and watch a movie. There's nothing more we can do until he calls."

"I don't have much of an appetite," Tess replied.

"Maybe just have a little nibble," Omar said.

Bobby took the cue and said, "Yeah, actually I could use something to eat myself."

"Me too," Jack said.

Tess shrugged. She turned to Omar. "Order something. What shall we watch?"

"Hmm, I was thinking *The Corpse Bride*. Too on the nose?"

She giggled. "You're too much. That sounds perfect."

***

Two hours later, Tess and Omar were sitting on the couch, laughing and having a sword fight with breadsticks from the takeout. Tess's phone rang. She looked at Omar like a lost lamb.

"It'll be okay," he said.

They got up and convened around her phone in the kitchen with Jack, Bobby, and another agent.

"Hello, Ray," she said. "Is it really you?"

"Hi, Essie," Ray said, his voice no longer disguised.

She shuddered. Jack rubbed her back.

"No one calls me that anymore," she said.

"I know, you go by Tess now. I'll have to get used to that."

"Ray, I don't understand why you're doing this."

"I needed to talk to you."

"You could have just called me. I would have talked to you."

"I needed you to see your husband for who he really is. I didn't think you'd listen to me. I needed to show you proof. I can't stand the thought of you with that guy. He's not who you think he is. He's not a hero."

"Ray, please just…"

"Listen to me," he interrupted.

"I am listening to you," she said.

"All I want is for you to see the truth. Then you'll realize you belong with me. You always have. I never should have let you go. I don't know how he talked his way out of the photographs I already sent, but you'll be getting another package any minute. Then you'll see."

Bobby motioned to the agent to go downstairs and alert the team to canvass the area.

"What did you send?" Tess asked.

"You'll see. Tess, it's going to hurt you, and please know that I'm sorry. I'll help you get over it. This was the only way I knew to get through to you."

"Ray, please. I'm happy in my life. If you're worried about me, you don't need to be. Jack is good to me. He treats me well. And you and I, maybe we can still be friends. Nothing has happened that can't be undone. I wish only good things for you."

"When you get the package, you're going to need some time. I understand that. I won't call back until tomorrow morning. I know that they're listening right now and trying to trace the call, but they won't be able to. After you see what I sent, get rid of them. Tell them you want them to leave. Find a way to speak to me privately tomorrow morning."

"You've made that impossible," Tess said.

"Just do it. I love you, Tess," he said, and he hung up.

Tess collapsed onto Jack. He wrapped his arms around her. "It's okay, baby. It'll be okay. There's something deeply wrong with him."

Twenty minutes later, Bobby returned to the kitchen holding a large envelope with Tess's name on it.

Jack stood up. Omar took a seat on the stool next to Tess.

"He left it at the house four doors down and rang the bell. Your neighbor was in the middle of feeding her baby, so she didn't get it until at least ten minutes later and then she needed to find someone to watch her kid. She just walked it over here. Our agents are scouring the neighborhood, but we think he's long gone."

Omar said, "So, how does one properly thank a neighbor for this? Are white lilies too morbid?"

Tess giggled. "Perhaps a fruit basket with a posthumous note that says, 'I'm dead, but thank you for being a good neighbor.'"

Omar chuckled. "That's perfect. She can watch it decompose."

Tess laughed.

Jack looked at Omar flatly.

"Sorry, just trying to lighten the mood," Omar said.

"Yeah," Jack muttered. He opened the envelope, pulled out two items, and inhaled deeply. "Sweetheart, I don't think you should see this."

"I want to know what's going on. We should all be on the same page."

Jack looked at her, a pained expression on his face. "I just don't want to upset you."

"Please let me see it," she replied.

"Bobby, can you give us a minute please?" Bobby left and Jack handed the items to Tess. The letter read: *Ask your husband who this woman is. He's a bad man. He doesn't love you.* There was a photograph of a woman.

"I don't understand. Who is she?" Tess asked.

"Sweetheart, she's a woman I met nearly ten years ago when I was deep undercover. She was an informant, and we, we were intimate."

"So, you're saying you were pretending to be someone else and you slept with her?"

"Yes."

She sat for a moment and said, "I understand. He's not calling back until the morning, so you don't need me, right?"

"Yeah," Jack said.

Tess stood up and started to walk away, her head lowered. Jack grabbed her hand. She didn't turn around. "It's fine. I understand," she said, letting go of his hand.

"Butterfly," Omar called.

"I'm fine," she said.

"Please, just wait a second," Omar said. He put his hands on her shoulders. "Look at me, Butterfly."

She raised her eyes.

He put his hands down and let her pass by.

As soon as she was gone, he turned to Jack and said, "She's not fine. Do you remember before you got married, I told you there was something fragile inside of Tess?"

He nodded.

"Imagine she has a small glass ball inside her heart. Even when her father died, even during that depression, she was able to protect it. Jack, I just looked into her eyes and I'm telling you, that fragile thing inside of Tess just cracked. You need to do something before it shatters."

"She knows I slept with other women before I met her."

"Even so, and I say this without any moral judgment whatsoever, this isn't exactly the typical way those things usually happen. But more importantly, it's something she didn't know about you and she just found out in the worst possible way. In her mind, this isn't about someone you slept with, it's something much bigger."

"What?" he asked.

"I can't say I know exactly what's going on in her head, but I'm sure this is feeding her biggest fear, which is that no one can ever truly love her. When she was a girl, do you know what that bastard used to say to her when he raped her?"

Jack shook his head.

"One of them never said a word, he'd just assault her and discard her. When the other one was done, he would say, 'No one will ever love you.' Can you imagine? I'm sure she felt that way even without his words, but this son of a bitch would actually say it to her, over and over again for years, obviously to silence her."

Jack clutched his head, fighting back tears.

"It's implanted deep within her psyche. Her greatest fear, perhaps her only fear, is that no one can really love her. It's one of the reasons she's struggled for so long to accept the adoration of her fans. She doesn't trust that it's real."

"She knows how much I love her," Jack said.

"Most of the time, yes," Omar said, looking down.

"What is it? Omar, you have to tell me."

"In over twenty years of friendship, I have never broken Tess's confidence. Not once. I'm going to break it now for the greater good, but Jack, if she ever finds out I told you this, it will do irreparable harm to our relationship."

"I give you my word, she'll never find out."

"Like I told you before, 99 percent of her believes she is worthy of love. That's because of you. But there's still that tiny voice. Most of the time it's dormant, but there are moments. Every once in a while, she'll be talking about you, always wonderful things, and then she'll look at me and say, 'Jack loves me.' Even though it sounds like a statement, she means it as a question. I always look at her and say, 'Yes, Butterfly.' Then her eyes get a little watery. I'm not sure if it's because she's relieved to have me confirm it, or because she feels guilty for having to ask. When she gets that way, I just say, 'Butterfly, it's okay.' Then she says, 'Please don't tell Jack.' I say, 'Of course not.' She smiles and we move on."

Jack's eyes watered and his mouth started to quiver.

"Jack, you're a wonderful husband and I know how much love you give her, but there's something inside of her that causes her to doubt that anyone can love her. It's not her fault or yours; it's because of what she's survived. Learning about Ray was traumatic enough. Nothing in the world is more important to her than you and what the two of you share. With how she's probably interpreted or twisted it in her mind, what he has revealed threatens that, and that's far worse to Tess than any threat on her life."

"What do you think I should do?" Jack asked.

"Well…"

Before Omar could respond, they heard a terrible commotion coming from the back door. Tess was screaming, "Get out of my way. Don't touch me! Get your hands off me."

Jack and Omar flew down the back staircase. Tess was trying to push her way past the two agents guarding the door. "I need some air," she screamed, hysterically.

"We can't let you leave, ma'am. We're under orders from Agent Miller to keep you inside the house," one replied.

"Tess," Jack hollered.

She didn't turn around and continued fighting with the agents. "He can't keep me here. I'm not a criminal. I haven't done anything. You can't keep me here," she shrieked.

Jack tried to reach out to her, but she flailed away. He stepped back. "Let me out," she bellowed again, more hysterically. "You can't keep me here. You can't do it."

The two agents stood in her way. One put his hand out to hold her back and she screamed, "Don't touch me! Don't touch me!"

"Don't touch her!" Jack commanded them.

They put their hands up, blocking the doorway with their bodies.

Bobby came racing around from the front of the house. "Let me through," he ordered the men. "Tess, what's going on?" he asked in a panicked voice.

"Bobby, Bobby, they won't let me out. They won't let me out," she wailed, tears streaming down her face.

He looked at Jack and Omar standing a few steps above, and then back at Tess. "It's okay, Tess. They're just trying to keep you safe."

"I need air. I need air," she begged.

"Try to calm down. It's going to be okay," Bobby said.

"Don't let them touch me. They have no right," she sobbed.

"No one's going to touch you," he said. He looked up at the agents. "Back off. We need some space. Everyone back off."

The agents took a step back. Jack and Omar each moved one step farther away.

Tess collapsed onto the floor. Bobby bent down in front of her. "It's okay, Tess. What can I do?"

"I can't breathe. I can't breathe," she gasped, beginning to hyperventilate.

"Just slow down. Slow down," he said calmly. "Try to catch your breath." He inhaled and exhaled slowly to show her. He repeated intentional breaths. She tried to mirror him, her breath gradually steadying.

"I need air. I can't breathe," she said more calmly. "They won't let me outside. I just want air," she said, staring into his eyes.

"That's because if you leave, we can't keep you safe," he replied.

"I don't care. I don't care," she said.

"Let's just sit for a minute. Let's just sit and try to breathe."

"Don't let me suffocate, Bobby. I don't care what else happens to me. Please, don't let me suffocate."

"I promise I won't. Just try to breathe, slowly."

Tess curled into a ball, her head down in her hands. She was trembling. A few moments passed before she looked up at Bobby. "I didn't do anything wrong. They can't keep me here. They can't force me."

"No one wants to force you, but we want you to choose to stay," he replied. He looked up at Jack and Omar, who watched in stunned helplessness.

Omar quietly said, "Butterfly, if they let you leave, they can't protect you."

Her eyes fixed on Bobby, she murmured, "I don't care."

Omar said, "The problem is that if you leave, Jack will follow you. We won't be able to stop him. Then he'll be in danger, too. I know you don't want that."

"Omar's right," Bobby said. "You know Jack. He'll go after you and then he won't be safe either."

She sat, taking deep, slow breaths, her body quivering. "Fine, I'll stay."

"Thank you, Tess," Bobby said. "Do you want me to walk you back upstairs? We can open a window so you can get some fresh air."

"I need a minute," she replied.

"Take all the time you need. I'm not going anywhere. There's no rush."

After several long minutes, she reluctantly said, "Okay, I'm ready."

Bobby motioned for Jack and Omar to go upstairs and then he helped Tess to her feet. She walked upstairs slowly, Bobby following behind. When they got inside, she said, "I'm going to my room to change."

"Butterfly, can I go with you?" Omar asked.

She shrugged.

"Tess, I'll be here if you need me," Bobby said.

"Thanks," she mumbled, and she trudged to her room, Omar in tow.

As soon as the bedroom door shut, Jack gripped his head with his hands and started weeping. "This is all my fault."

"No, it isn't," Bobby said, putting his hand on his shoulder. "There's one asshole responsible for this and we're going to get him."

"I hurt her," Jack said, trying to muffle his crying.

"Jack, Tess has told me countless times that you're the best thing that ever happened to her. Nothing has changed that. The only reason she came back inside was because she loves you and wants to protect you. This is an intense, traumatic situation. It's not your fault and she'll be okay. We all love her. We're all working to make sure she comes out of this okay."

Jack sniffled, trying to regain his composure. The bedroom door opened and Tess emerged in gray pajamas. Jack looked at her, but she turned the other way.

"Tess is going up to her office," Omar said in a hushed tone. He motioned for Jack to follow behind.

When they got upstairs, Omar signaled for Jack to wait. He stopped on the stairs and leaned against the wall, holding his head in his hands, trying to ground himself. A few minutes later, Omar returned. "Go be with her," he whispered.

"Thank you," Jack replied.

He entered the large room and found Tess sitting on the oversized window seat, her legs outstretched. She was gazing out the window, smoking a cigarette. He walked over to her.

Still staring out the window, in a barely audible voice, she said, "Does Omar think I need a babysitter? I told him I'm not going to jump. It's either too high or too low, depending on one's goal."

He let out a huff. "Can I join you?"

"Sure," she said, scooching closer to the window. He sat beside her.

"Please don't talk," she said.

"Okay," he replied, and he took a cigarette and lit it.

Eventually, she stamped out her third cigarette and leaned against Jack, burrowing into him. He put his arm around her.

"I smoke sometimes," she said softly.

"I know. When you're sad or when you have writer's block. You hide them in the false bottom of the window seat."

"Yeah."

"I know you, Tess."

"Must be nice."

"Tess…"

"I'm sorry. Forget I said that."

"Please, can we talk about this?" he asked.

"It doesn't matter," she said.

"Yes, it does. Sweetheart, do you think I did something bad to that woman? Because it was consensual, I would never…"

"Jack, I know. I would never think that."

"I'm sorry I didn't tell you. When we met, I tried to tell you everything I could about the things I'd done for work, things I've wrestled with. I never wanted anything to surprise you. It didn't even occur to me…"

"Jack, I'm not upset with you."

"It's okay to be angry with me. Please just tell me," he replied.

"I've never been mad at you. Not once. Not for a minute since we met."

"Tess, you haven't looked at me. You haven't made eye contact with me even for a second. Are you horrified by what I've done? Is it repugnant to you? It's okay if that's how you feel."

She started crying. "No, please stop saying things like that. It tortures me that you think that. I've told you so many times that I'm proud of you and everything you've done to keep the people in this country safe. It isn't anything like that. It's not you. It's me."

"Sweetheart, what is it? It's killing me to see you in pain and that you can't even look at me. Why won't you look at me?"

"Because I'm afraid that if I do, you'll break my heart. I'm afraid of what you'll say if I tell you how I feel. I'll see it in your eyes if you lie to me."

"You always say, 'The only way out is through.' Please, baby, just look at me. You can tell me anything. There's nothing we can't get through together. I'm not going to hurt you."

She wiped her face, sat up, and slowly raised her eyes until they met his.

"I know what I'm about to say is going to sound crazy to you, but I can't help it."

He put his hand on her cheek, gently caressing her skin and wiping away her remaining tears. "It's okay. Tell me."

"What we have means more to me than anything. Every minute we've spent together has mattered to me. And I can't fake anything; I don't lie or pretend, ever. Every minute I've spent with you has been real for me. But you... you can pretend anything. And I just don't know if..."

"If I've ever pretended anything with you?"

She nodded.

"Oh sweetheart, no, never, not for a single second. Tess, you mean more to me than anything in the world. What I have with you is the best thing I've ever had in my life. Nothing has been more real. I would do anything to protect what we have. Nothing else matters but being with you. I love you with my whole heart, forever. I promise you."

"Really?"

"Yes."

"Show me."

He took the back of her head in his hand and kissed her passionately. "Come here," he said. He led her to the couch at the far end of the room, grabbed a throw blanket from one of the chairs, and unfurled it over the couch. He pulled Tess's shirt over her head and then pulled his own shirt off. He ran his fingers gently along the sides of her face, and then delicately traced the curves of her body. "I love you so much," he said, and he began kissing her, tenderly but with intention. They made love with their eyes locked onto each other. After, they lay entangled on the sofa. Jack grabbed another blanket and draped it over them. "Tess, what we have is so special."

"I know. I'm sorry. I don't know what's wrong with me."

"There's nothing wrong with you. You're perfect just as you are. We're a team, an unbreakable team. There's nothing we can't deal with together. You have my heart forever. Promise me you know that. Promise me you believe it."

"I do," she whispered. She rubbed his cheek. "Jack, I love you so much."

"I love you, too. More than I could ever tell you."

"Can we stay up here until the morning? I don't want to go back down there with everyone. I just want to be alone with you."

"Of course," he said.

She put her head on his chest and he ran his fingers through her hair until they fell asleep.

CHAPTER 10

Tess and Jack woke up early the next morning, stiff from sleeping on the office sofa. "What time is it?" Tess whispered.

"I don't know, but the sun's up. We should probably go downstairs."

"Okay," she said.

"Wait, let me hold you for a minute more, just like this."

A few minutes later, they got up, put their clothes on, and headed to their bedroom. "It's a little after six," Jack said.

"Let's take a shower," Tess replied.

After they showered, Jack shaved and got dressed. "I'm going to see what's going on."

"I'll be out soon," Tess said, fixing her makeup.

Jack went into the kitchen, where Omar and Bobby were drinking coffee.

"How's Tess?" Omar asked.

"She's better, much better. You were right, but we worked it out. Thank you."

"Good. Did you guys get any sleep?" Omar asked.

Jack nodded. "Believe it or not, it was actually peaceful." He turned to Bobby and said, "Please tell me you've got him."

"Jack, everyone's been working around the clock. I've been up half the night. We can't find this guy. We think the best thing to do is have Tess make a plan to meet him. That may be the only way we can flush him out," Bobby said.

"Absolutely not," Jack replied.

"With any luck, we can nab him before he ever gets close to her," Bobby said. "You know how this works, and you must know that it's our only play. Some guys never get caught."

"We're not using Tess as bait. These things can go wrong. It's out of the question," Jack insisted.

"I'm with Jack," Omar said. "It's too dangerous."

"This guy knows how to hide," Bobby said.

"We're not doing it. Don't even think about suggesting this to Tess," Jack said, just as Tess strolled into the room.

"Don't even think about what?" she asked.

Omar stood up and pecked her on the cheek. "You look good, Butterfly. How are you feeling?"

"I'm fine. What were you talking about?"

"We're just trying to strategize," Bobby said. "Batting around ideas."

"You still haven't found him?" she asked.

"Not yet, but we will," Bobby said.

"Take a load off and have some coffee," Omar suggested.

She plopped onto the stool next to him. Jack poured her a mug of coffee and brought it to her.

"Thank you, baby."

He kissed the top of her head. "Do you want something to eat?"

"Sure, thanks."

She sipped her coffee and then turned to Bobby. "He said he's going to call this morning. I think we should do what he said. Don't try to trace or record the call. I can try to convince him I'm alone and see if I can get him to meet me somewhere. That way, he'll have to come out into the open."

Bobby looked at Jack and then back at Tess. "We considered that, but it's just too risky."

"Well, if you don't find him, I don't understand how else this is going to end. We can't live like this indefinitely. We all need to get back to our lives, which will be difficult with him on the loose and threatening me."

All three men exchanged looks.

"Oh, I see," Tess said. "Jack doesn't want me to do it."

"Sweetheart, it's too dangerous. There's no telling what he'll do, and we can't guarantee that you'll be safe. That's not a chance I'm willing to take."

"Well, I'm sure everyone will do their best to keep me safe. I don't see what other choice we have. Besides, I honestly don't think he wants to harm me."

"Tess, you're not doing this. I won't allow you to be put in a perilous situation. We'll get him some other way," Jack said.

She walked over to him. He leaned against the counter and lowered his head. "Baby, look at me," she said. He raised his head. "You said we're a team. You can't make this decision alone. I want to do this so we can get on with our lives. He's not going to hurt me, no matter what he says. You have to trust me."

"Sweetheart, please…"

"Jack, Bobby's your friend so I'm sure he's saying what you told him to say. Am I right? Is this what they think we should do to end this nightmare? Tell me the truth."

"Yes, but I've been a part of countless operations like this, and things can go wrong. This guy is unstable and threatening your life. I don't want you at risk."

"I know you don't. I'm not completely thrilled about it either, but it's the only way to end this. Please, Jack. Let's do this. I can handle it. I'll be fine. I know him. Part of me would like to have some closure, and that will only come from seeing him. Something went wrong in his life. Maybe I can help him. Please."

Jack inhaled. "This goes against every instinct I have. You have to do exactly what we tell you to do."

"I will."

"I'll be there the whole time."

"I don't want you there; then you'll be in harm's way, too. There's a whole team of people who can handle this. You don't need to be involved," she said.

"Tess, it's not up for negotiation. If you do this, I *will* be there."

She gazed into his eyes, nodded, and kissed him to seal the deal.

"Omar, what's the appropriate attire for meeting with my stalker slash possible assassin?"

"How about a straitjacket to go with this insane idea?" he quipped.

"I do love a buckle," she said with a giggle.

Omar smirked.

"Come on, play with me," Tess whined. "What shall I wear?"

"Oh, I don't know, running shoes and a gun holster," he replied.

"Definitely not black, that's like full surrender."

"Nor white, it's like giving him the middle finger."

"Perhaps navy?"

"Yes, navy says, 'I hope to live, but I'm prepared to die.' Plus, you look fabulous in navy."

She smiled. "Good point."

Omar's expression turned serious. "Butterfly, you don't have to do this."

"I'll be fine. I refuse to live like a hostage for another day. Let's have some breakfast and we can plan what I should say when he calls. Jack, what are you making for my last meal?"

He shook his head. "This isn't funny. I'm terrified, Tess."

She sprang up and rushed over to him, taking him in her arms. "I'm sorry, baby. We're joking, it's just what we do. We all understand the gravity of the situation, but being gloomy isn't going to help. I'm just trying to lighten the mood. I didn't mean to be insensitive. Let's make a heaping pile of eggs. They symbolize life and rebirth. I'll help."

"Okay," he said.

***

"When he calls, put it on speaker but try to convince him that you're talking to him privately. Speak quietly, as if you're taking the call secretively. The meeting place has to be public, like a shopping center or busy park. The later, the better. We need as much time as possible to get our people in position before he arrives," Bobby said.

"Okay," Tess replied.

"You'll be wearing a wireless micro-listening device. We'll have our eyes and ears on you the whole time."

"I'm sure you'll do your best," Tess said.

Promptly at eight o'clock, Tess's phone rang. Jack sat on the stool beside her with his hand on her back, and then gave her the signal to answer.

"Hello?" she said softly.

"Are they listening to us?" Ray asked.

"No. I turned the ringer off so they wouldn't know when you called."

"Did you get my package?"

"Yes. It was devastating." She looked at Jack and he rubbed her back.

"I'm sorry. I had no choice."

"I need to see you in person," she said.

"There's a park six blocks north of you," he said.

She looked at Jack and he nodded.

"Yes, I know it," she said.

"Meet me there at 10:45. Sit on a bench on the south side."

"That's too soon. I don't know if I can get rid of them that quickly. I need a little time to talk my way out of the house alone."

"10:45, Tess. You'll find a way."

She looked at Jack and he nodded.

"Okay, I'll try," she said.

"I love you, Tess. I'll see you soon." He hung up.

"Come here," Jack said, embracing her.

"You did great, Tess," Bobby said.

Jack said, "I don't like that he was so specific about the time. There's a reason."

"He's got to know that Tess is working with us, or that even if she isn't, we may follow her. He must have some diversion planned so that he can make it to her without giving us a chance to grab him," Bobby said. "Jack, the guy's CIA. He knows what he's doing, but we'll have an army there. It will be okay."

Jack said, "The south side of the park has a playground and some public restrooms. Tess, we need you to sit as far away from the playground as possible."

"Okay," she said.

Jack turned to Bobby. "We can get a sharpshooter on the roof of the restrooms."

"I had the same thought," Bobby said. "We can position undercover agents in the men's room and at the picnic tables."

"A sharpshooter?" Tess asked. "Jack, promise me you're not going to kill him."

"Sweetheart…"

"Promise me, Jack. No one is dying today."

"Tess, we'll do everything we can to use nonlethal force," Bobby said.

"Everything will be okay," Jack said, rubbing her back. "We need to get the team ready. Will you be all right with Omar for a while?"

She nodded.

"Oh yes, we'll have oodles of fun picking out a tasteful outfit for the day's festivities," Omar said. "Come on, Butterfly, let's go have a fashion show."

Tess stood up, kissed Jack, and followed Omar to her bedroom.

***

An hour and a half later, Omar shuffled into the kitchen, leaned against the refrigerator, and put his face in his hands. Jack and the other agents were engrossed in conversation. Jack noticed Omar and asked, "What's wrong?"

Omar slowly raised his head. "She thinks she's going to die."

Bobby took the unspoken cue to clear the room. "We're all set here," Bobby told the other men. "Everyone needs to go join the advance team and get in position." He turned to Jack and lowered his voice. "I'll be downstairs if you need anything."

As soon as the room cleared, Jack turned to Omar.

"She called her estate lawyer to make sure her will can't be contested, and then she sat me down to review her wishes for her books. She insisted that she was just being responsible and that even people going in for minor surgery do these sorts of things, but…"

"Tell me," Jack said.

"Then she made me dance with her to 'Your Song,' our whole *Moulin Rouge* routine." He started to cry. He sniffled and continued, "She whispered in my ear, 'Jack is the love of my life and you are my soul mate.' Then, she said, 'Thank you,' like it was the last thing she was ever going to say to me."

Jack ran his hand through his hair and closed his eyes. "Maybe she's just a little scared."

Omar shook his head. "I don't think so. Tess doesn't get scared, she becomes resolved. I toured with her in the Middle East when she had all kinds of serious death threats. She was detained by men holding machine guns, and even then, she wasn't like this. I think she's planning to sacrifice herself. If things go badly and you're in danger, or even if Ray is, I think she'll try to protect either of you at her own expense. You know how she is. She always thinks of others before herself. Her best qualities will betray her in this situation. You heard her: when you reviewed the plan, her first concern was that Ray should live. She said she wants to help him."

He paused and took a breath. "I know Tess better than anyone. Hell, I probably know her better than myself. But the one thing I've never known is the extent to which she values her own life, if at all. I honestly don't know. When you two got back from Hawaii, she told me about riding on a motorcycle with you and I asked her if she wore a helmet. She said she did because you made her. Think about that, Jack. You had to tell her to wear a helmet."

"Tess always lives in the moment. Maybe she just doesn't think about things like that."

"Yeah, maybe. But are you sure? Sure enough to wager her life?" Omar asked.

"I didn't want her to do this in the first place. She insisted," Jack said.

"I know," Omar muttered.

"I don't know what to do. I don't think I can stop her from going through with this," Jack said.

"You can't. But Jack, she can't do this with a mindset that it's okay if something happens to her, that she's an acceptable loss. Please talk to her. She needs to know we need her to live."

Jack nodded and headed off to see Tess. When he opened the bedroom door, she was sitting in a chair in the corner of the room, putting her shoes on.

"Hi, honey. I'll be right there," she said.

He walked over and knelt on the floor in front of her. "I need to talk to you."

"Yeah?" she said.

"Omar said you called your lawyer."

"Jack, people do that when they're having their appendix out or for any number of reasons. I would have discussed it with you, but I saw no reason to upset you more than you already are. If something were to happen…"

"Tess," he interrupted. "I don't want you thinking that way."

"I'm sure I'll be fine, but honey, even aside from Ray, I'm going to be surrounded by men with guns. That's not an everyday circumstance. No one can know with certainty what will happen."

He put his hand on her cheek and she leaned into it. "Sweetheart, if something happens to you, I will never recover. Omar will never recover. That's how much you mean to us. You need to protect your life as if it were mine or his, because that's how it feels to us. You are the most important thing in our world and I will not survive a world without you in it. Do you understand?"

"Yes," she whispered.

"Promise me."

"I promise."

They stood up, kissed gently, and walked hand in hand into the kitchen where Omar, Bobby, and Joe were waiting.

"Tess," Joe said.

She walked over and hugged him tightly.

"Jack and Bobby have been keeping me apprised of what's going on. I'm so sorry about this horrific ordeal. I wanted to see you before you go. Please, can we chat?"

"Of course," she said, and they both sat down.

"Tess, I've told you before that you're the most impressive person I've ever met."

She smiled.

"You once told me that the key to negotiation is crafting a narrative and believing in it."

"Yes," she said.

"No one is better at that than you. No one. Your instincts are laser sharp. Have your story ready, Tess. Have your story and believe it to your core, and I know you'll make it out of this."

"That's good advice. Thank you."

He leaned over and hugged her. "I'm going to wait at the house with Omar. We'll be here when you get back."

She smiled and patted his hand.

"Everything is set up. I think we should get the listening device on Tess and go," Bobby said.

"Wait," Omar said. "Butterfly, please come here."

She walked over to him and he put his hands on her shoulders. "Come what may," he said.

"*Moulin Rouge*," she whispered.

"Our special film. I was thinking about the scene when Satine is going to sleep with the duke. She's going to sacrifice herself for everyone else, but she remembers her special song with the man she loves and she can't go through with it. It reminds her to save herself."

"Yes," she said.

"That's what we need you to do," Omar said. "Do you understand?"

She nodded.

He clasped her tightly and whispered, "Don't forget that and you'll be fine."

She took a deep breath and walked over to Bobby. "I'm ready."

Jack placed the small transmitter on her. "We'll hear everything that happens. Remember to pick a bench as close to the restrooms as possible. Don't look around at any of our people. They'll be watching you, but you can't watch them. He knows what I look like, so I'll be hidden. You won't be able to see me, but I'll be nearby."

"I understand," she said.

"I don't want you taking any chances, but if you see an opportunity to safely move away from him, we need you far enough that we can either move in or take a shot. If that's what you're thinking, say something so we'll know."

"Come what may. I'll say, come what may." She winked at Omar.

Jack kissed the top of her head, and then he, Tess, and Bobby went down the back stairs. Tess headed to her car in the garage and the men headed out the back door.

***

Tess sat on a bench near the restrooms, rubbing the locket around her neck. At 10:48, a bus pulled up on the street in front of her. She noticed a large group of children and a few adults step off. As she watched the children, she saw Ray, wearing a baseball cap, walking in the middle of the crowd, children all around him. As they ran past Tess's bench on their way to the playground, he quickly sat down beside her and pressed a gun into her rib cage.

"I've waited for this for so long. You look beautiful," he said.

"Ray, you don't need the gun."

"I know you're not alone. You brought them here with you, didn't you?"

"I told you I would come alone."

"They may have followed you, even if you don't realize it."

"Ray, please put the gun away."

"Don't be scared. I would never hurt you. But I have to be sure."

"You're hurting me now. Holding a gun to me hurts me. Please, let's just relax and talk."

"Don't focus on it. I'll make it up to you, I promise. I saw your picture in the newspaper a few months ago. I couldn't believe that you married someone like me after all."

"You really don't know anything about him. He's not like you. Everyone is different. Just because two people have the same job, doesn't mean they're the same type of person."

"Forget about him. You never should have been with him in the first place. I should have fought to get you back years ago. I just didn't think you would end up with someone like me. I loved you before you were Tess Lee. I loved you for the girl you were. You can trust me."

"Ray, if I can trust you, then show me. Please put the gun down. You don't need it."

"Don't focus on that. Let's just talk."

"What do you want to talk about?" she asked.

"Do you remember all the good times we had?"

"I do. I remember everything."

"I'll never forget that night I was driving you home in the pouring rain and that Journey song you loved came on. You made me pull over and blast the radio on full volume. You got out and stood in front of the truck, in the glow of the headlights, dancing in the rain. You were sopping wet when I dropped you off."

She smiled. "I remember."

"What else do you remember, Tess?"

She stroked his cheek tenderly. "I remember how sweet you could be."

"And you were fearless. Remember that lake we used to go to on hot summer days? You would climb on that rope swing and leap into the freezing water. You'd do it over and over again, laughing the whole time. None of the other girls were like you."

"Then we'd swim out to that old wooden dock," she said.

He smiled.

She continued, "I remember one day especially, one of my favorite days. When we climbed up onto the dock, I got that awful splinter in my foot. You said you'd get it out. I was squirming because it hurt so badly, but you rubbed my leg and told me to look into your eyes. Then you pulled it out. We sat as you massaged my foot until I couldn't feel any more pain. We lay on that dock for hours, just the two of us, watching the sky turn from dusk to night, and the stars suddenly filling the vast blue," she said.

"You were obsessed with that twinkly star. I said that there were thousands of them, but you just watched that one twinkle for hours. Do you remember, Tess?"

She nodded.

"I begged you to tell me why you would only look at that one twinkling star, but you wouldn't. Tell me now. Why, with the sky lit up with thousands, were you focused on how that one twinkled?"

She shook her head. "I don't think I have the words to explain it."

"Maybe someday you will," he said.

She touched the side of his face again. "I promise you I'll try to find the words."

He smiled. "When it started to get late that night, I asked if you were cold, just lying there in your bathing suit. You said no, and that you didn't want to leave. You wanted to stay as long as possible. I knew then: you were my girl. I have always loved you."

"I know you did," she said.

"We used to kiss for hours."

"We were teenagers."

"Kiss me now, Tess."

She shook her head. "I'm not doing anything with that gun pressed up against me."

"Kiss me so I know how you feel, and then I'll put it away."

"If you don't put the gun down, I'm going to leave, come what may," she said.

"You can't. I have a gun."

"Then you better be prepared to use it. I know you don't want to," she said, caressing his cheek. "I know you don't want to hurt me. Ray, I'm going to slowly stand up and I'm going to start walking away. If you put the gun down, I'll stay and we can talk longer. I'm getting up now."

She slowly rose, the gun still against her. He stood up alongside her.

"Don't walk away, or I'll shoot you."

"No, you won't. You don't want to hurt me. We used to listen to the frogs and watch the stars. I know you, Ray Potter, and all the goodness inside of you. I trusted you then and I trust you now. I trust you no matter what anyone says. Do you understand? I trust you no matter what anyone says. You could never hurt me. I see it in your sweet eyes, just like when you were a boy. Please put the gun down," she said, as she slowly took a step backward.

"Don't leave me," he said, as she took another step backward.

"Just put it down. Please, Ray. Put it down," she said, taking another step backward.

He began to lower his arm. "Okay, Tess. I'll put it down."

She smiled. "That's it, just put it down," she said, taking another step back.

Suddenly, a shot rang out and Ray toppled over. Tess collapsed onto the pavement and burst into tears. Agents swarmed from every direction. Jack dove onto the ground and grabbed her. "It's over. It's over, sweetheart. You're safe," he said. She clung to him, sobbing. "It's okay, baby. You're okay," he said, holding her tightly.

"Will Ray be all right?" she whimpered, not daring to look at him.

"Yes. They shot him in the arm to subdue him. It's not serious."

"I was afraid if I moved away from him, they would kill him, but I remembered what I promised you."

She pulled back and looked at him. He held her face in his hands and said, "I was so scared. I love you so much."

"I love you, too."

"How did you know he wasn't going to shoot you?"

"I didn't, but I believed."

He cradled her in his arms and they wept together as the emotion of the day washed over them.

***

Tess and Jack arrived at their house to find Omar and Joe waiting as promised.

"Oh, Butterfly, thank heavens you're okay," Omar said, throwing his arms around her.

"I love you," she said.

"I love you, too. Was it awful?"

She stepped back. "It was sad. Really sad."

"Bobby called and filled us in," Joe said. "You were very brave, Tess."

"I took your advice," she replied.

"Thank God it all worked out. I'm so sorry you had to go through this," he said.

"What can we do?" Omar asked. "How about some hot tea?"

"Sure," she said.

"I'll help Omar. You two go sit in the living room," Joe said.

Jack took Tess's hand and they sat on the couch. He put his arm around her, and she nuzzled into him. He started gently massaging her head. "Don't stop. That feels so good," she said.

"Sweetheart, we can stay like this for the rest of our lives if you want."

She turned to him and pressed her mouth to his. "I couldn't kiss him," she whispered.

"I know."

Twenty minutes later, they were all finishing their tea when Bobby arrived. He was as white as a ghost.

"What is it?" Jack asked.

Bobby knelt on the floor in front of Tess and Jack. "Tess, Ray is dead."

"What?" she asked, sitting straight up. "Jack said it was a minor wound."

"It was. He committed suicide. In the ambulance, he somehow got a hold of something sharp and stabbed himself in his carotid artery. He bled out before he made it to the hospital. I'm so sorry. Also, you should know that his gun wasn't loaded. It was just for show. There weren't any bullets."

She was silent as tears cascaded down her face. She turned to Jack. He looked into her eyes and then pulled her close. "Oh sweetheart, I'm so sorry. I'm so sorry."

Eventually, she leaned back, four sets of loving eyes upon her. "Butterfly, what can we do?" Omar asked.

She sniffled and turned to Joe. "Will you do me a favor?"

"Anything, Tess."

"I know you all see Ray through the lens of these last few days, but I knew him for years. He was good to me. Something happened to him along the way. You have access to information. Please, find out whatever you can."

"Okay. I will," Joe replied.

"Thank you." She stood up. "Excuse me. I need to take a shower and wash away this awful day, and then I think I'll lie down."

"Sweetheart, I'll come join you in a few minutes," Jack said.

As soon as Tess was out of earshot, Jack turned to Omar and asked, "Do you think she'll be all right?"

"Eventually. This must be devastating for her. The more she leans on you, the better. But you know how she is, she never asks for anything for herself and tends to withdraw when she's hurt. She needs to learn to share her feelings and say what she needs," he replied.

Jack let out a huff. "Do you know what she did when she first got to the park? There was a homeless woman, and Tess stopped to give her money and hold her hands. She was on her way to meet Ray, but first, she stopped to help a stranger. Bobby and I just looked at each other dumbfounded."

"That's Tess. She never loses herself and she always cares more about others," Omar replied.

"When she was speaking with Ray, she was so kind to him. I knew it was genuine. I was terrified that she might sacrifice herself to protect him. I was so relieved that she didn't. I wanted that bastard dead, but I was glad that we didn't kill him because I knew what that would do to her. There was a moment when I knew with certainty that I loved her more than I hated him. It was like something dark inside me finally lifted because of her. Now this…"

"It's horrible, but you'll get her through this. She has a remarkable ability to transform darkness into light. With that gift and how she feels about you, I don't think there's anything she can't survive. It just may take a little time."

"Jack, I'm going to go into the office to do what Tess asked. I'll come back as soon as I have anything. Maybe it will help her find some peace with this," Joe said.

"Thank you. I'm going to go be with Tess. I know you guys need to get home to Clay and Gina. You can let yourselves out," Jack said.

"No way. I'm staying here. I'll be here as long as you two need," Bobby said.

"Me too," Omar said. "Go be with Tess. We'll hang out and watch TV or something."

"I guess there's no point in arguing," Jack said. "Thank you."

When Jack got to their bedroom, he heard the shower running. He knocked on the bathroom door and then walked in. Tess was crumpled on the floor of the shower, the water pounding down on her head. He kicked off his shoes, got into the shower with his clothes on, sat down, and wrapped his arms and legs around her. She nestled into him. "I'm so sorry, sweetheart. I'm here. I'm here and I'm not going anywhere."

CHAPTER 11

Tess and Jack lay in bed for hours, their arms around each other, no words spoken.

Out of the blue, Tess whispered, "Do you know how lucky I feel to have you?"

"I'm the lucky one," he said softly.

"Jack, I know you think I don't care about my life, but I need you to know that I do. You told me to protect my life as if it were yours or Omar's. You must think I don't care if I live, but I do."

"It's just that you always put everyone else first, and sometimes I see a glimmer of something so delicate, so sad in your eyes. I'm scared to death that you don't know how much I need you."

"Jack, I do love life, and it's not because of you or Omar. I love it just for what it is, all the tragedy and beauty. I try not to think about the past or the future, just each moment as I live them. But when I was sitting on that bench, my mind flooded, as if every moment in time was alive at once, and I promise you I wanted more, especially more moments with you. There could never be enough moments with you," she said, caressing his arm.

"Tess, these past few days have been the most terrifying of my life. When you said, 'Come what may,' my heart stopped."

"That's because you weren't looking into his eyes. If you were, you'd have known he couldn't have pulled that trigger. I'm not surprised the gun wasn't loaded. I never believed he wanted to hurt me."

"You took such a big risk."

"I was trying to save myself, and Ray, too."

He squeezed her. She crawled on top of him, they gazed into each other's eyes, and kissed slowly.

"Tess, I know this has been awful, but I need you to do something for me."

"What?"

"Let me help you. Trust me. Whatever you feel, whatever you need, it's all okay. Do you understand?"

She nodded, leaned down for another kiss, and then rolled onto her side. "You are the most beautiful man I've ever known. The deepest part of my soul feels completely safe with you."

"Never doubt that," he said.

***

When Tess and Jack emerged from their room, Omar and Bobby were unpacking bags of takeout.

"We figured you two must be starving. Butterfly, there's no clear-cut takeout option for situations in which one escapes her gun-toting ex-boyfriend and then mourns his suicide, so we went with Chinese. That seems to be what you Americans resort to when you don't quite know what to do with yourselves," Omar said.

She smiled. "That's perfect."

"We got extra chopsticks, because I know you think it's a crime to eat Chinese food with silverware."

"It is," she replied.

Omar kissed her forehead. "How are you, really?"

"I don't know."

"Well, that seems reasonable."

"Why don't we bring all of this into the living room?" Tess suggested.

They were halfway through their meal, listening to Bobby tell a hilarious story about his in-laws at Tess's request, when Joe returned.

"Come, take a seat. We have loads of food," Omar said.

Joe handed Tess a manila folder. "This is everything I could get. I hope it helps you."

She stood up and hugged him. "Thank you so much."

Joe sat down and Tess looked around the room. "I don't know how I got so fortunate to have so many wonderful men who care about me. I don't have the words to tell you how much I love you all and how deeply I appreciate everything you've done for me." Her eyes began to tear.

"We love you, Tess," Bobby said.

"Anything you need," Joe added.

Omar stood up and put his arms around her. "You are my soul mate forever and always. You make this life extraordinary."

She kissed his cheek and then faced Jack. "I'm going up to the office to read this. I need to do it alone."

He nodded.

When Tess left the room, Bobby looked at Joe and said, "Grab some food."

He picked up a plate and helped himself.

"What did you find?" Jack asked.

"There's no one thing, no defining event that I could find, but there were patterns. His father treated his mother badly: affairs, gambling, domestic violence that was covered up. He was passed over for several promotions and honors. In each case, he contended that rule breakers were rising past him. There was an incident just a couple of years ago when he was a part of an undercover operation, where an informant he was close to was killed. The woman had been sleeping with another undercover agent, and Ray blamed him. There was an internal investigation and the matter was dropped. My overall impression was that he felt like he never got what he deserved, and although he had a sense of women being mistreated, he didn't quite process it right. I thoroughly reviewed the interview with his ex-wife and I think, in his mind, Tess was the best thing that ever happened to him and he blamed himself for not trying to win her back. Tess is famous, so he would always hear things about her. My guess is that when he saw the photo of you two in the newspaper, he researched you and decided that Tess had ended up with a lesser version of himself, the kind of man he'd been fighting his whole life."

Jack looked down.

"He was wrong, Jack. Like I said, he didn't process things correctly."

"Thanks."

"Hopefully, this will give Tess some peace of mind. Who knows, maybe she'll see something in there that I missed."

***

An hour later, Jack went up to the office.

Tess was sitting on the window seat, gazing outside and clutching the folder. She turned and smiled. "Hey."

"Hey, sweetheart. I just wanted to check on you."

"Come here," she said, sliding closer to the window to make room for him.

He sat down and put his arm around her. "Did it help?" he asked, gesturing at the folder.

"Maybe. A little. Did Joe tell you what it says?"

"Yes."

"It's so strange. I never knew about the stuff with his parents, and I never told him anything about my family. But what I said to him today was true. That one summer day, out on the dock, was one of my only happy memories from that time. Neither of us wanted to leave. I didn't want to go home and now I realize he didn't either. Maybe that's why we were so close. We both lived with violence, sadness, loneliness, and trauma. I guess he was never able to shake those things. Life can be terribly unfair, which is why it's so important to focus on that for which we can be grateful. I've tried to do that my whole adult life. It's why I search for light. When I read the file, it seemed like he wasn't ever able to do that, like he only focused on the unfairness, the darkness."

He took her hand.

"Jack, I need to write my way through this." She looked at him and said, "Did you know that when we got married, some of my fans were worried that I wouldn't write the same way anymore because I was happy?"

He brushed the side of her face and touched his forehead to hers. He pulled back and she continued. "Omar thinks I don't know about that; he's always looking out for me. But there are fan websites and things online. I try to avoid them, but sometimes I see things. What they don't understand, maybe no one does, is that the reason I'm able to have any happiness is because I have some place to put my pain. Just because you fall in love doesn't mean all of your hurt magically disappears."

"I know," he said softly.

"I know you do," she said, caressing his cheek. "Everything that's happened has given me an idea for my next novel. It came from something Ray and I talked about. He asked me to explain something that I didn't have the words for, but I think I do now. I know it sounds crazy, but I'm going to give myself one week to write it."

"Well, that's great sweetheart, but doesn't it usually take you at least six months?"

"Yes, but I don't have the heart for a long project. I need to see if I can just get it out." She paused and said, "Jack, will you do something for me?"

"Anything."

"Can you stay home this week? If I'm alone, I think I'll be too sad. I just want you here, near me, while I write. I know it's silly and I don't want to be a burden and…"

"Don't finish that sentence. You could never be a burden. Yes, of course I'll stay with you. I would be honored."

He leaned over, kissed her, and smiled brightly.

"What is it?" she asked.

"I'm just so happy that you asked. You don't usually tell me what you need. It's what I've always wanted."

"I trust you and I'm sorry if I've ever made you feel like I don't. It's not you, it's me."

"I already told you, you're perfect just as you are. Never apologize to me. You are and will always be the love of my life."

"And you're mine."

CHAPTER 12

Tess woke up like a bolt, screaming. Jack sprang up and threw his arms around her. "It's okay. It's okay, baby. I've got you," he said, holding her heaving body.

She latched onto him and he held her tightly, her breath fast. Eventually, she steadied herself and whimpered, "Did it really happen? Is Ray dead?"

"Yes," he whispered.

"Is it my fault?"

"No, sweetheart. It's not your fault. It's no one's fault."

After a moment passed, she asked, "What time is it?"

He craned his neck to look at the clock. "It's just after four."

"Go back to sleep," she said, slipping out from his arms.

She got out of bed, put her robe on, and went to the bathroom. A few minutes later, she emerged.

"Where are you going?" Jack asked.

"Upstairs. Go back to sleep."

Tess went up to the office and turned the lights on. She brushed her fingers along her laptop and meandered over to the window seat. She stood, looked out at the dark sky that was waiting to become light, and inhaled deeply. She walked back to her desk and put on her reading glasses. She turned her computer on, opened a new document, and began typing. Ten minutes later, Jack came into the room carrying two mugs of coffee. Without a word, he put one down on her desk, kissed the top of her head, and dropped into a reclining chair across the room. Tess looked at him for a long moment, her eyes smiling, and then resumed typing.

***

Three hours later, Jack walked over to Tess and massaged her shoulders. "I'm going to get some breakfast and see if the Sunday paper was delivered. Can I get you something to eat? I could make your oatmeal."

"No, thank you."

"I can bring it up here if you want."

"I'm fine. I'm not hungry. Thank you," she said, typing.

Soon, Jack returned with the large newspaper. He stopped at Tess's desk, kissed her head, and quietly said, "If you get hungry or you need anything, just let me know."

"Thank you, baby."

Tess wrote for hours. Every once in a while, she'd get up to stretch or use the bathroom. At one point, she paced around the room murmuring to herself. Then she went into her secret cigarette stash, lit one, and sat on the window seat with outstretched legs. She made room for Jack when he came to join her.

"Taking a break or blocked?" he asked, lighting a cigarette.

"Working something out," she replied wistfully.

After they stamped out their cigarette butts, Tess took Jack's hand, kissed it, and whispered, "I love you." She returned to her laptop and continued working.

A little while later, Jack said, "Sweetheart, it's after noon. You've been up since four and you haven't eaten a thing. What can I get you?"

"I'm okay," she said. "More coffee would be great."

When Jack returned, he came carrying a mug of coffee and a plate with cheese, crackers, nuts, and dried fruit. "Just in case you change your mind," he said.

He was about to walk away, but she grabbed his hand and said, "Thank you."

"My pleasure."

He returned to his recliner and turned on his iPad, occasionally glancing over at Tess. Eventually, she picked up a piece of cheese and ate it, followed by a dried apricot, and then another. He tried to mask his smile. An hour later, he came by to ask if she wanted more coffee. The plate was empty.

***

As afternoon turned to evening, Jack said, "I'm going to get a workout in and then jump in the shower."

"Okay, honey," Tess said, continuing to type. An hour later, she heard him heading downstairs from the gym toward the first floor. She got up and followed him. She meandered into their bedroom just as she heard the shower start. She took off her clothes, walked into the bathroom, stepped into the shower, and slipped her arms around him.

He turned around and kissed her lips and neck. After their shower, he dried her off from head to toe before drying himself. He wrapped a towel around her and she whispered, "Be with me, Jack."

He picked her up and carried her to the bed. "Be gentle," she said. They made love tenderly and then lay in each other's arms.

"Jack, is it terrible that I feel happy?" she asked.

"No, baby," he said, holding her close. "I'm happy, too."

"I need to get back to my book," she said.

"How about dinner first? I can make that spicy spaghetti you like, or we can order takeout."

"Spaghetti sounds perfect."

"You go work and I'll call you when it's ready. If you're too in the zone to step away, I'll bring it up to you."

"Thank you."

Half an hour later, Jack hollered, "Tess, dinner's ready."

"On my way," she called.

Jack had set the dining room table with candles, a bottle of sparkling water, pasta, and salad. "Right over here," he said when she walked in, pulling out the chair adjacent to his.

"You didn't have to go to all this trouble," she said.

"It wasn't any trouble. Every bit of time we have counts and I don't want to waste a minute of it."

"I love you so much," she said.

"I love you, too, sweetheart."

***

Tess slurped her last strand of pasta as Jack finished telling her a riveting story about an undercover operation he was once involved in.

"Do you ever miss that kind of work?" she asked.

He shook his head. "I did that for a long time. Now I'm just glad to have a life of my own. Our life together, it's everything to me."

"To me, too," she said, standing up and picking up her plate.

"Leave that," he said. "I'll clean up."

"I can help," she said.

"Sweetheart, you've been taking care of me since we met. I'm thrilled for the chance to take care of you. I know you want to get back to writing."

She smiled. "Honey, I'm just going to sleep upstairs on the couch tonight, maybe for the week. I need to be able to keep working and nap when I need it."

"I'll stay up there with you."

"There's no reason for you not to sleep well. I'll be fine. Thanks again for dinner. It was scrumptious, both the food and the conversation."

"My pleasure."

Twenty minutes later, Jack walked into the office holding a sheet, a comforter, and pillows. Tess smiled at him, tears in her eyes. "I figured if we're going to sleep up here this week, we should at least make it more comfortable," he said.

"I love you more than words."

He smiled. "I'll be over there watching the game with my headphones."

Jack fell asleep on the couch around eleven o'clock. Two hours later, Tess joined him. She got up the next morning at six, brushed her teeth, and sat back down at her laptop. Jack brought her a cup of coffee and a bowl of oatmeal. For the next two days, they continued like this: Tess writing and Jack by her side.

Wednesday night, just before midnight, Tess joined Jack on the couch.

"Hey, sweetheart," he said. "How's it going?"

"I'm almost done. I think I only have a day or so of writing left. For a first draft, at least."

"Wow, that's great."

"It's just flowing out of me, like it's always been there, waiting to be released."

He kissed her forehead.

"Would you mind if I went to see Omar tomorrow morning for our usual Thursday breakfast? I know he's worried about me."

"Of course not."

"Jack, thank you for what you've done for me this week, and what you always do for me. I don't have the words to tell you how much it means to me. I appreciate and love you more than you could ever know."

"I do know, Tess. You show me every day. I'm always here for you, anything you need."

"Jack, I was thinking about what you said about every minute counting. When you were exercising earlier, I contacted the owner of the Maui property to see if they're interested in selling. It's ours if we want it. We can even have the staff. And of course, we can buy a Harley."

"Are you serious?" he asked.

"We could use it for vacations, or go back and forth, or just be permanent beach bums. It depends on how you feel."

"Baby, I'll quit my job tomorrow if you really want to do this. I'll need to work again, at some point. I need to be of service. But there's consulting I can do wherever we are, and I'd love to do some volunteer work for vets."

"Maybe we could just buy it and play it by ear. Spend time there, spend time here. The LA house is in between, so we could even spend time there," she said.

He kissed her passionately. "That sounds blissful, sweetheart."

"You know, if you're going to quit your job, we could spend more time in Asia. We could go for as long as we want. I could even do a worldwide book tour and we could hop from continent to continent. We could stay at this wonderful little hotel I know in Stockholm that overlooks the water. And my favorite painting in the entire world is in Paris. I'd love to show you."

"Which one is your favorite?"

"It's a painting Claude Monet did of his wife on her deathbed. It's not the painting I love so much, but the signature. He signed all his artworks exactly the same way, except for that one. He actually never signed it when he was alive. Maybe it felt too final, or maybe he just wanted to keep the painting for himself. After he died, it was stamped with his signature. There's a heart in his name. It's the most beautiful, romantic, heartbreaking thing. I cry every time I see it. Simple things can be the most extraordinary. It's rare that something so perfectly expresses our feelings."

He smiled. "I would like to see that. And if we're really going around the world, I've always wanted to go to Australia. I'd love to take you snorkeling and scuba diving. Have you ever been?"

"Yes, but I haven't done those things, and I haven't seen any of it with you."

"Come here," he said, pulling her on top of him. "I love you so much, Tess. I don't care where we are, only that we're together."

"When that house in Maui is ours, do you know what I'm looking forward to the most?"

"The outdoor shower?" he asked, kissing her neck.

"Well, that too. But I was thinking about riding on a bike with you, just feeling and breathing the boundless sea air. Just being with you in the sunlight and breathing."

***

When Tess got home from breakfast the following day, Jack was sitting in the kitchen, working on his laptop.

"Hi, sweetheart. How's Omar?"

"He's great," she said, walking over to kiss him. "He and Clay are so happy. I was thinking that we should invite everyone over here tomorrow night for our usual Friday get-together, but we could surprise them and make it an engagement celebration, you know, just for our group. I feel so badly that all this drama stole their thunder. I think I'll be done with the novel by then."

"That's a great idea. I'll text everyone. I can try to get a caterer if you want."

"Let's order from that Mediterranean place they love. Maybe you could pick up some champagne and red velvet cupcakes from the bakery; they're Omar's favorites."

"Sure," he said.

"What have you been up to?"

"Sorting through some work stuff. I want to help get things in order before I bail on them."

She smiled. "I'm heading upstairs."

He picked up his laptop and said, "Coming with you."

Tess wrote furiously all day, stopping only to eat dinner with Jack. At ten o'clock, she hit print. She picked up the manuscript and plunked down next to Jack on the couch.

"It's done?" he asked.

"Uh huh. A novel in five days. It might be crap, but I don't think so."

"Amazing. What's it about?"

"Me, Ray, you, our friends, but none of us either. It's about the things that haunt us, the things we focus on and can't let go of, the doubts we carry. It's about learning to breathe through the tragedy in our lives until we can see that pain is just love in disguise. I don't know, it's hard to explain."

"What's the title?"

"*Ray of Light.*"

He smiled and put his hand on her face.

"Jack, will you read it?"

"I'd be honored."

"Here," she said handing him the manuscript. "Turn to the second page. It's kind of my Monet, except I want to express how I feel now, while I'm here on this planet."

He flipped to the dedication page, which simply read: *For Jack.*

"This book was inspired by my love for you, the strength and safety you give me, and the light you bring to my world, so every word is for you. I love you so much," she said.

"I love you with my whole heart, forever."

"I'm exhausted. Let's go to sleep."

"You go ahead. I'm going to start on this."

"Oh Jack, it's late and I know you must be…"

"I'll see you down there later," he said.

***

Tess was asleep when Jack crawled into bed. She woke up and whispered, "What time is it?"

"Just after three. I couldn't stop reading."

She turned to face him, wiping sleep dust from the corners of her eyes.

He swept the hair out of her face, tucking a strand behind her ear. "Tess, it's the most beautiful thing I've ever read."

"Really?" she mumbled.

"It's so honest, so painfully sad, and incredibly hopeful. I'm in awe. I can't believe you wrote that in five days. I've always known you had a gift for transforming darkness into light, but this, this is just, I don't even have the words."

She smiled.

"And it made me feel like I know you even better. These last few days have been so special. Thank you for telling me how you felt and what you needed. It meant the world to me to be there for you. We're as close as two people can be."

She burrowed into his chest and whispered, "I know."

CHAPTER 13

Tess was setting the final serving spoon on the buffet when Bobby, Gina, and Joe arrived.

Bobby gave Tess a huge hug. "How are you doing?" he asked.

"Really well."

"I'm so glad."

"Thank you for everything."

"Nah, that's what friends are for."

"Here's the banner," Joe said to Jack.

"Thanks for picking it up. Let's hang it before they get here."

"Oooh, that looks great," Tess said.

"Tess, can I help with anything?" Gina asked.

"I think we're all set. We'll save the bubbly for when they get here. Can I get you a drink in the meantime?"

"Just sparkling water, please."

Tess raised her eyebrows.

"We're trying again," Gina said.

Tess smiled and embraced her. "That's wonderful. I know it will happen for you."

"Who wants a beer?" Jack asked.

"Me," Bobby said.

"Me too," Joe said.

They drank and chatted until the doorbell rang. Jack answered it, ushering Omar and Clay inside.

"Surprise!" everyone shouted.

"What's all this?" Omar asked, looking up at the banner that read: *Congratulations Omar and Clay*, surrounded by hearts.

"Just a little engagement celebration," Tess said.

"That's so sweet. Thank you," Clay said, hugging her.

"We're thrilled for you both," she whispered. "You've made him so happy."

Clay scanned the buffet and said, "Oh, you got my favorite artichokes. What a treat."

Tess smiled. "Please, everyone help yourselves to some food and get comfortable in the living room. The champagne is waiting."

"Uh, Butterfly, do I get one of those hugs?" Omar asked.

She threw her arms around him, squeezing him tightly. "You can have all the hugs."

"Thank you for this," he whispered.

"Love should be celebrated. You and Clay are made for each other. I know you'll be blissfully happy."

They hugged for what seemed like an eternity before pulling apart. "Well, that's enough of that," Omar said, wiping the corners of his eyes. "So, Butterfly, a novel in five days? Your publisher will be delighted. It seems we haven't been getting the most out of you all these years. Even if we let you have weekends off and the occasional vacation, we can get what, fifty a year? Chop, chop. Better get to work."

Tess giggled. "It just poured out of me. But don't get too excited, Tess Lee might be taking a sabbatical."

"Yes, I hear congratulations are in order for you two. You got the house in Maui."

"We made them an offer they couldn't refuse. It happened quickly," Jack said.

"Well, I'll be sure to wear out my welcome in your guest quarters," Omar replied.

"Not possible," Tess said.

"Oh, I'll give it my best effort," Omar replied.

"Well, you can be exhausting. Come to think of it, I don't know how Clay will put up with you. Perhaps I should have a chat with him," Tess said.

They both laughed.

"You two are so funny together. How long have you been friends?" Gina asked.

"About twenty-two years," Tess replied.

"That's right," Omar said.

"Do you ever fight?" Gina asked.

"We had one argument back in college. I was cross with her about something, but I can't even remember what. It was probably something stupid. I spoke harshly to her. When I saw the melancholic look in her eyes, I knew I never wanted to see that look again. We haven't argued since. Some people simply must be cherished."

Tess smiled. "I'm very lucky he's put up with me all these years."

"Yes, you are. It's certainly been tiresome," Omar joked.

Tess giggled. "You're lucky we're not at the bar. I would have lobbed a pretzel at you."

He grabbed her and knuckled the top of her head.

"And see, now I have bad hair. This is what I put up with," she said. "Come on, Gina. Let's join the others in the living room."

"Jack and I will be there in a minute," Omar said.

"All right," Tess replied.

Omar motioned for Jack to come to the far side of the kitchen, and he lowered his voice. "Something amazing happened yesterday. I was going to call you, but I wanted to tell you in person. When Tess and I were having breakfast, she was talking about you and said, 'Jack loves me.' But she said it like a statement. Resolute. I just smiled and then she smiled and we continued on with the conversation."

Jack teared up.

"I looked into her eyes, and I swear something was different. It was like something inside her was finally at peace."

"Thank you," Jack sniffled, wiping his eyes.

"You know, I really always did want Tess to fall in love, but there was a small part of me that worried that after so many years of it being just the two of us, it would be hard to share her. It's easy to share her with you, Jack."

Jack smiled. "It's also easy to share her with you. I promise that no matter where we go or where we live, I won't allow anything to come between the two of you."

Omar smiled. "I know. Thank you."

***

"That was delicious," Omar said, taking the last bite of his cupcake. "You were so sweet to get red velvet."

"Jack picked them up. I know how you love them," Tess said.

"There's another box in the fridge for you and Clay to take home," Jack said.

"Butterfly, will you tell us about the new novel? Jack said it's a masterpiece."

Tess blushed. "Jack isn't objective."

"That may be true, but it's incredible," Jack said, leaning over to kiss the side of her head. "Why don't you read them a little?"

"We would love that," Joe said.

"That would be such a treat," Gina said.

"No pressure or anything, but we all want to hear it," Bobby added.

Tess smiled. "All right. Honey, would you get the manuscript? You can pick a passage for me to read."

"With pleasure," Jack said, standing up.

"Omar, while he's getting it, I did want to mention something to you. I'll publish it, but I don't want to sell the entertainment rights or do any kind of licensing that breaks it up into pieces. I just want it to live as a novel. Let's keep it pure."

Omar smiled. "Of course, Butterfly. Anything you want. What inspired you to write this latest tome like a mad author chained to her computer?"

"When I was a teenager, Ray once asked me a question I didn't know how to answer. It wasn't that I didn't want to, I just didn't know how. He asked me the same thing when we were sitting on that park bench. I still didn't know how to answer, but I promised him I would find the words. I just wanted to keep my promise."

Jack returned with the manuscript. He flipped through it and pulled out a page. "This is my favorite bit; the whole novel is contained in this one part," he said, handing it to Tess. She smiled. He sat in the corner of the couch and she leaned back onto him.

"I guess I should give you a little context," Tess began. "The protagonist is depressed. One summer night, she goes to her favorite lake, jumps into the freezing water, and swims out to an old dock. As she's swimming, she's trying to decide if she'll ever swim back, or if she'll drown herself. This is how the scene goes:

"She pulled herself up onto the old wooden dock, her body cold and dripping. 'Damn it,' she muttered at the splinter lodged in the palm of her hand. Crawling to the middle of the dock, she collapsed on her back, trying to catch her breath. She rubbed her fingers across the sore spot in her hand, knowing there was no way to remove the shard in the dark night. How is it, she wondered, that something so small could hurt so much? If she removed the splinter, would she always feel its absence? It was something that was inside of her that will forever be missing, like that piece of herself she had lost long before she got to know it, or that other piece that was stolen, or that other piece she sacrificed for reasons she no longer remembers.

"Her mind flooded with things she didn't yet understand: the relationship of the small part to the whole, the haunting nature of the one out of one hundred, the loudness of the single voice that did not praise us amid the sea of those that did, our obsession with the one love we lost and not the boundless possibilities for love we might find. Above all, she wondered about the nature of doubt, how it creeps in and casts a shadow over the light, causing us to ask: Does he truly love me? Do I deserve love? Am I worthy? Perhaps these questions would never be answered. On this night, there was only one question that mattered: Will I swim to shore or will I suffocate in the ghostly waters? Until she had an answer, she would stay there. She looked up at the night sky, bursting with stars. One twinkling star caught her eye. It drew her gaze as if it were the light at the end of the proverbial dark tunnel. The twinkle pulsed like her heartbeat. Mesmerized, she blocked out all the others and watched her lone star twinkle. Was it a lifeline, an anchor, or a distraction? She wondered: If she could lasso that one star and pull it to her, would the entire sky crumple like a piece of paper? Would it give her a paper cut that would then be all she felt? Overwhelmed, she squeezed her eyelids shut and opened them again. This time, she saw all the stars lighting up the sky. She inhaled deeply, oxygen filling her lungs. Breathe, she told herself, just breathe."

EPILOGUE

Five Months Later

"I'm so excited to show you Japan," Tess said, holding Jack's hand as they waited at passport control, wearing matching aviator sunglasses. An assistant stood behind them with their luggage.

"I can't stop thinking about Paris," he said, leaning over to kiss her cheek. "The city of love, the city of lights. Those are the things that always remind me of you: love and light. It was magical. I didn't want to leave. And you speak French so beautifully."

"It was so romantic being there with you, sitting in quiet corners of little bistros, talking for hours. The sunshine in the mornings when you'd tickle me in bed. Those sexy nights in our hotel, the moonlight on your face. Every minute with you. I felt like I had never been there before."

Jack smiled. "I never really knew much about art until I met you. Going to those museums and seeing the art through your eyes was incredible. I loved the Musée d'Orsay, especially that Monet with his heart signature. I used to see so much darkness, with just rare glimpses of the good stuff. Now, it's the opposite. Tess, I see everything differently because of you," he said, stroking her hair. "Thank you for showing me the world through your eyes. I love you more than I could possibly say."

"I love you, too."

"Welcome to Tokyo, Ms. Lee," the passport control officer said, waving them through.

On the other side of the control office, Tess stopped. "Baby, it's usually a little hectic when I arrive in Asia. Europe is much more low-key. When we walk through that door, Ambassador Kaito Harada will be waiting to greet us, along with my Japanese publisher, Riku, and our translator and driver. There are usually fans waiting to take photos and get their books signed. Riku always informs the media about my arrival to promote the book signings, so it's possible they'll be waiting for us, too. I'll have to do the Tess Lee thing."

Jack pressed his lips gently to hers. "Do your thing."

She smiled, but didn't move.

"Do you need a minute or are you ready, Mrs. Miller?" he asked.

"Kiss me again."

He kissed her softly.

"Now I'm ready." She signaled to their assistant to open the door.

As they stepped out into the arrivals area, they saw a mob of people waiting behind a barricade and media standing to the right. The fans started screaming and cheering when they saw Tess, photographers snapping away. Kaito, Riku, and the translator quickly approached them. They all greeted Tess warmly and she introduced Jack.

"The reporters would like to ask you some questions. I told them to keep it brief, as you've had a long journey," Riku said.

She took off her sunglasses and handed them to her assistant. "First, let me greet the fans who have been so gracious to come and wait for me. I'd like to sign their books."

Riku handed her a black Sharpie. "Certainly. I will inform the press," he said.

Tess walked right up to the barricade. "Thank you so much for this warm welcome to Japan, one of my favorite places to visit." She started hugging fans, signing books, and taking countless selfies. Some fans were so overcome that they began to cry, telling Tess what her books mean to them. Jack stood back, watching with a look of pride on his face. After ten minutes, she promised to come back after speaking with the media to sign any books she had missed. She stepped back. Her translator stood beside her and Riku signaled to the camera crews.

"Ms. Lee, welcome to Tokyo," the first reporter said. "You last visited Japan five years ago. Why has it been so long and why have you returned now?"

"I took a few years off from public events to focus on writing and my personal life. I got married and I've been enjoying spending time with my husband," she said, glancing at Jack. "I've only just resumed international travel, and Japan was at the top of my list of places I wanted to visit. Japan is one of my absolute favorite countries in the world and I can't wait to share it with my husband. The people are so gracious, and the sights are breathtaking. Meeting readers here has always been special for me, so I'm looking forward to my book signings. I'm grateful for this incredibly warm welcome. Thank you."

Riku called on another reporter.

"Ms. Lee, for the first time in your career, you released two novels within a matter of months. They are both beautiful and bear your signature style, exploring life's deepest challenges and reminding us there is hope on the other side. Your newest novel, *Ray of Light*, is currently number one in Japan. How would you describe that book?"

"Thank you for your kind words. For me, *Ray of Light* is about the pain we cause ourselves when we doubt, when we feel unworthy, when we are unable to fully accept love. For some of us, it's the hardest thing to do. We can't change the audio feed in our head, screaming or whispering that we are not enough. Doubt is easy. Where there is light, doubt can waft in like a cloud of darkness, casting a shadow over everything. When we start to believe in ourselves and accept unconditional love, we allow a ray of light to enter that darkness, and if we lean into it, soon there is only brightness."

Riku faced the media and said something in Japanese. Tess's translator whispered, "He said there will be only one more question before you continue signing books for your fans."

Tess smiled.

"*Ray of Light* is dedicated to your husband. Does it hold a special meaning to you?"

"What my novels mean to me is something I keep private. My relationship with each book is very personal." She paused for a moment, craned her neck to look at Jack, and smiled. "But I will tell you that my husband is my family and I could not have written it without him. I mean that in every possible way. And for that reason, it will always hold an immeasurably special place in my heart."

SUGGESTED CLASSROOM OR BOOK CLUB USE

1. What do you think about Tess and Jack's relationship? What is special about their relationship, and why is their bond so strong? What role does past trauma play in their love story and how they choose to treat one another?
2. *Twinkle* explores the nature of doubt in close relationships. How do Tess and Jack navigate this issue?
3. The friendship between Tess and Omar is the other primary "love" story in this novel. What do you think about their relationship? What does this relationship say about the families we choose to create? Can you draw comparisons between this friendship and any of your own?
4. How do the characters communicate with each other? Consider the verbal and physical aspects of their communication. What do their patterns of interaction reveal about their relationships?
5. *Twinkle* suggests that love, in its many forms, can help us heal. Explore this theme in relation to any of the main or supporting characters. What does unconditional love look like in this book?
6. The issue of coping with sexual abuse and trauma is central to the story. What do we learn from Tess's experience? What can we learn from the ways her loved ones help her?
7. Popular culture is filled with examples of toxic masculinity. While negative male forces lurk in the shadows of *Twinkle* (e.g., Dick Clayton, Ray, Tess's abusers), the primary characters exhibit positive masculinity. Discuss this in relation to any of the characters (Jack, Joe, Bobby, Omar, Clay, and/or Abdul).
8. Building on the last question, when Tess's life is being threatened, Jack falls into dark patterns of masculinity. What does he learn through this process? How does Tess help him?
9. The relationship of the small part to the greater whole, or the 1 percent to the 99 percent, is a theme in *Twinkle*. What are some examples? What's the purpose of this theme?

10. *Twinkle* is a book about love. What is the overall message about love? Find some examples that support your position.

CREATIVE WRITING ACTIVITIES

1. Bobby, Joe, Gina, Clay, Abdul, and the president are supporting characters. Select one of these characters and write their story.
2. Select one of the characters and look ahead five years. Write a short story based on where you think they end up.
3. If *Twinkle* were a play instead of a novel, it would likely include monologues by the main characters. Select a character and write their pivotal monologue.
4. In the final chapter, Tess reads from her latest novel, *Ray of Light*. Use this scene or imagine a different part of the novel to write an original short story.
5. Write an alternative ending to *Twinkle*.

QUALITATIVE RESEARCH ACTIVITIES

1. Select several scenes and perform discourse or conversation analysis on the dialogue. For example, use one of the conversations at Shelby's Bar, a conversation between Tess and Jack, a conversation at the gala, or any other exchange.
2. Research sexual assault and locate peer-reviewed articles or scholarly essays on related issues (e.g., rape culture, family abuse, gender and violence, trauma). Use your findings to write a paper, using Tess's experiences to illustrate or challenge your research.

ART ACTIVITIES

1. Create a visual or audiovisual version of the scene that Tess recites from her novel, *Ray of Light*.
2. Respond artistically to *Twinkle*. Using any medium – literary, visual, or performative – create an artistic response to a theme in the novel or express how the novel made you feel.

AUTHOR Q&A

How would you describe Twinkle?

It's a love story that explores the nature of doubt in our lives and relationships. It's a deeply human experience for people to think, on some level, that they aren't enough. This belief causes so much pain. The characters in this novel use love to confront this innately human fear and help one another learn to more fully love themselves and those around them.

As a follow-up to Shooting Stars, *this is the second Tess Lee and Jack Miller novel. What inspired you to keep writing about them?*

I absolutely love these characters, not only Tess and Jack, but all of their friends. Of all my books, these characters are nearest and dearest to me. When I finished *Shooting Stars*, I knew there were more stories to tell and I hoped readers would enjoy following their journey as much as I love writing about them. I'm using these characters to explore love, to write a love letter to love, one that will unfold over several books. *Shooting Stars* explored love and healing. It also had a theme of darkness and light. These themes are still a part of *Twinkle*, because the characters are who they are, but this is a new exploration. *Twinkle* explores love and doubt, and investigates the relationship of the small part to the greater whole. If *Twinkle* is your introduction to these characters, see how Tess and Jack met, in the first chapter of *Shooting Stars*, reprinted at the end of this book.

Does this mean you'll write more books about Tess and Jack?

Yes. There are five completed books in total. There is a clue near the end of each book about the topic for the next one. I'm absolutely in love with the third novel in the series and I can't wait to release it. It includes my favorite line I've ever written, and the ending brings me to happy tears.

What can we expect from the rest of the Tess Lee and Jack Miller novels?

Each novel explores love at the intersection of another topic. Each novel also has its own theme, linked to that exploration. The characters are who they are, so healing, trauma, grief, and loss resurface, as do themes of darkness and light. There are a few things I can promise you: Every novel opens with a scene featuring just Tess and Jack; this is, after all, their love story. Every novel concludes with an epilogue, which could be set anywhere from a day to a year later. Each epilogue ends with Tess speaking, because she is our heroine. Tess and Jack will always love each other, although each book contains a dramatic event that will test them. While new characters may appear, the friends you've gotten to know are an important part of all the novels and we learn more about the back stories of these relationships as we progress. Each book also includes an excerpt from one of Tess's novels. I've tried to balance drama with humor in all the novels, so there's a mix of tearful moments and those that make me laugh out loud. In these ways, I hope the books balance darkness and light, mirroring the very story they will ultimately tell.

What do you hope readers will take away from this book?

We are enough, exactly as we are. We need to breathe into who we are and breathe into love. Sometimes, truly accepting love is the hardest thing to do, whether it's from a lover, friends, family, or even the art we experience, but accepting it brings the greatest rewards. Breathe. Just breathe.

SHOOTING STARS, CHAPTER 1

"How's your son doing in school?" Tess asked the bartender.

"Really well. He especially loves the history course he's taking."

A man came in and sat two stools down from Tess. They looked at each other and smiled in acknowledgment.

"Hey, Jack. The usual?" the bartender asked.

Jack nodded. "Please."

Tess continued chatting with the bartender as he served Jack a bottle of beer. "The humanities are so important. It's a shame they're undervalued," she said.

"You're the expert," the bartender replied.

Just then, a different man sidled up to Tess. "You have the most beautiful brown eyes," he said.

"Do I?" she asked.

"And the way your hair flows all the way down your back. You know what they say about dirty blondes?"

"I don't think you should finish that sentence," Tess said.

"I've been watching you. Can I buy you a drink?" he asked.

"No, thank you," she replied.

"Come on, just one drink. I'm a nice guy."

"No, thank you," she said, turning away.

The "nice guy" opened his mouth to protest, but Jack stood up with an imposing air and said, "The lady said no."

The man huffed and walked away.

"Thank you," Tess said.

"Don't mention it. I did feel a little sorry for him, though. You are beautiful and I can't blame him for taking a shot."

Tess smiled and pulled out the stool next to her. "Please, scooch over. Let me buy your drink."

He smiled and took the seat next to her. "My name is Tess Lee," she said.

"Jack Miller," he replied. "But it's on me. Yours looks nearly empty. What are you having?"

"Sparkling water. I don't drink. It's just a personal choice," she replied.

"Another sparkling water for my new friend," Jack said to the bartender. "So, Tess, what brings you here by yourself?"

"I was supposed to meet my best friend, Omar, but he had a last-minute emergency. His partner, Clay, was pulled over tonight and it became an incident."

"What was he pulled over for?" Jack asked.

"Being Black," Tess replied. "Clay is a surgeon and was on his way home from the hospital. He was pulled over for no reason and harassed. It's happened to him before. Once, he was on his way to an emergency at the hospital, and he was detained even after he showed his hospital ID. It's egregious. Anyway, I told Omar to stay home with him. They need time together to process and decompress. I was already in a cab on my way here, so I decided to come anyway. I moved to DC from LA about six months ago and I don't have that much of a life yet, I suppose. And you?"

"My friends ditched me. We usually get together on Friday nights at a different bar, but they all had to stay late at work. This place is right down the block from my apartment."

"So, what do you do?" she asked.

"I'm a federal agent with the Bureau, working in counterterrorism. I joined the military right out of high school, Special Forces. I was in the field, often deep undercover, until about a year ago, when I took a desk job as the head of my division."

"Wow, you're like the real-life Jack Bauer. You even look a little like him, with that whole rugged, handsome, hero thing you have going on," she said.

He blushed. "I promise you I'm no Jack Bauer, even on my best day. People thought that character was so tragic, but the real tragedy is that Jack Bauer doesn't exist and you're stuck with guys like me."

She smiled. "What made you choose that line of work?"

"My father was in the military and then became a firefighter. The idea of service always seemed important. I wanted to serve my country, to protect people. It's hard to explain, but when I see someone innocent being threatened, I'm willing to do whatever is necessary to protect them. I know it sounds cliché, but I feel like it's my purpose in life."

"That's noble," she said.

He shook his head. "The lived reality often isn't. When you spend most of your life in the abyss, it gets pretty dark."

"A residue remains, right?" she asked.

He looked at her intently, a little surprised. "Yes, exactly."

"I understand. You convince yourself it's all been for something that matters more than you do, that whatever part of yourself you sacrificed was worth it, because it simply has to be."

He looked at her as if she had read his innermost thoughts. "Yes," he said softly. "Tell me, what do you do?"

"I'm a novelist."

"What are your books about?" he asked.

"That's a hard question to answer. I guess I wanted to write about everything: what it means to live a life, why it's so hard, and how it could be easier. Perhaps my goals were too lofty, and in that respect, each book fails more spectacularly than the one before."

The bartender smirked.

Tess wistfully said, "Maybe reality can never live up to our dreams."

They continued talking, completely engrossed with one another. Two hours later, Jack said, "I live nearby. Do you want to come over for a cup of coffee?"

Tess looked him straight in his warm, blue eyes. "I'd love to."

Jack threw some money down on the bar to cover both tabs. The bartender said, "Ms. Lee, are you sure you're all right? I can call you a cab."

"You're very kind, but I'm fine. Thank you."

Jack opened the door and held it for Tess. "Do you know the bartender?"

"Just met him tonight," she replied.

"Down this way," Jack said, taking her hand as if it were completely natural. They approached a homeless man on the corner asking for money. Tess walked right up to him, pulled a twenty dollar bill from her pocket, and handed it to him. She held his hand as she passed the bill, looked in his eyes, and said, "Be well."

As they walked away, Jack said, "That was really sweet, but you should be more careful."

"I trust my instincts," she replied.

When they arrived at Jack's small apartment, he took her coat. She glanced around and noticed the walls were completely bare. "How long have you lived here?" she asked.

"About nine years," he replied. "Can I get you some coffee or something else to drink?"

She shook her head and meandered over to his bedroom. He followed. He took the back of her head in his hand and started to kiss her, gently and with increasing passion. He pulled off his shirt and they continued kissing. He pulled back to look at her and she noticed the scars on his body: two on his right shoulder, another on his abdomen, and smaller marks along his upper arms. When he noticed her looking, he turned around to lower the light, revealing the gashes across his back. She brushed her fingers along the deep marks. "I'm sorry," he said. "War wounds. A couple of gunshots. Some other stuff from when I was in the Gulf. I know it's gruesome."

"It's wonderful," she whispered.

"What?" he said.

"I'm sorry, I didn't mean it that way. It's just that I've never seen anyone whose outsides match my insides."

He looked at her sympathetically.

"I was abused when I was little. My grandfather and my uncle. It started when I was eight. No one can see my wounds, but they're there."

He stood still, looking at her.

"I'm so sorry. I've never shared that with any man I've been with in my entire life, and I just met you. That has to be the least sexy thing ever. I'll leave," she stammered, trying to walk past him.

He took her hand and pulled her back toward him. He cupped her face in his hands, gently caressed her cheeks, and kissed her. They made love with their eyes locked on to each other. Afterward, he held her in his arms and said, "That was so special. Spend the day with me tomorrow."

"Okay," she replied, and they fell asleep, their limbs entangled.

***

The next morning, Tess awoke to find a note on the pillow beside her that read, "Went to get breakfast. There's an extra toothbrush on the bathroom counter. Back soon."

She brushed her teeth, and by the time she was done, Jack had returned.

"Hey, sweetheart," he said, as if they had known each other for years. He pecked her on the cheek. "I didn't know what you like so I got bagels, muffins, and a fruit salad. Do you want coffee?"

"Yes, please."

He poured two mugs of coffee and they sat down at the small table. "What kind of food do you like, anyway?" he asked.

"I'm a vegetarian. I don't believe in hurting living beings."

Jack looked down.

"Innocent beings," she said.

He smiled. "I guess that's why you're so tiny."

She started picking at the fruit salad. Jack noticed that she was moving it around with her fork, almost like she was counting. He looked at her quizzically.

"I'm weird with food. I don't eat that much. It's kind of a control thing," She paused, keeping her eyes on her breakfast. "I have problems."

He reached across the table and put his hand on hers. "That's okay. We all have problems. They make us human."

They spent the day together, talking, watching TV, and walking around his neighborhood. They got Chinese takeout for dinner and made love twice more. Sunday morning, Tess realized she'd missed a dozen calls and text messages from Omar. She called him while Jack was making coffee.

"I promise, I'm fine. I'm sorry I worried you. I met someone. His name is Jack. He's special… Well, if he is holding me hostage, don't pay the ransom. I want to stay… I'll text you all about it… Okay, love you, too. Bye."

"He was worried about you?" Jack asked.

"He's been looking out for me for a long time. We talk every day, but I guess I was too preoccupied yesterday," she said, slipping her hands around his waist.

"Sounds like a good friend," Jack said.

"He's more than that; he's my family. He moved here a year ago and convinced me to leave LA so we could be in the same city. But enough about him. Right now, I'm only interested in you. Come here," she said, walking backward toward his bedroom. Just as he was about to touch her, she grabbed a pillow and walloped him.

"Oh, you're in trouble now," he said, darting for a pillow. They tumbled onto the bed, laughing.

They spent the rest of the day lounging around Jack's apartment, reading the Sunday newspaper, and sharing stories. That night before they went to sleep, Jack said, "I don't want the weekend to end. Do you have to work tomorrow?"

"Well, I do work for myself. Can you take the day off?"

"I once took two weeks off, but other than that, I've never taken a single day off in over twenty years. So yeah, I think I'm due for a personal day."

***

The next day, Tess and Jack went for a walk and ended up at a local park. They sat on a bench, huddled together in the chilly, late autumn weather. Suddenly, a little boy ran over and tugged at Tess's coat sleeve.

"Do you have superpowers?" he asked. "My dad says you do."

"Excuse me?" she said.

His father came running over. "I'm so sorry if he was bothering you, Ms. Lee."

"Not at all," she replied with a gracious smile.

"I'm a librarian. I want to thank you for everything you've done," he said.

"My pleasure," she replied. "Thank you for what *you* do."

The little boy tugged at her sleeve again. "Well? Do you have superpowers?"

His father laughed. Tess looked at the boy and lowered her voice conspiratorially. "I'll tell you a secret. Everyone has superpowers, they just don't know it."

"Even me?" he asked.

"Especially you," she replied.

Jack smiled.

The man took his son's hand. "I think we've bothered these people enough. Thank you again, Ms. Lee," he said, leading his son down the path.

Jack looked at Tess. "That was so sweet, what you said to that boy."

She leaned over and kissed him.

"What was the deal with his father? It seemed like he knew you."

"I did some volunteer work for the library a few months ago," she replied.

A few little girls came skipping past them, drawing their attention.

"It's starting to get cold. You want to go to a movie?" Jack asked.

"Sure."

After the movie, they went to a neighborhood Italian restaurant for dinner. The maître d' greeted Tess like an old friend. "Ms. Lee, such a pleasure. We have our best table for you."

"I guess you've been here before," Jack said as he pulled out her chair.

"Jack, listen to the music," she said.

"Sinatra – the best."

"Let's dance," she said.

He looked around. "I don't think they have dancing here."

"But I love to dance," she said.

He stood up, took her hands, and they danced by the table. "You know, I'm not much of a dancer, but I promise to dance to as many slow songs as you want."

"Maybe someday we'll have a special song," she said, nuzzling into his chest.

Later, when they got back to Jack's apartment, he led her to the couch with a slightly serious look. "I need to tell you something."

"What is it?" she asked.

"You've seen the scars on my body, but there's another side of it. Tess, I've done things – things that may be unimaginable to someone as sweet as you, things I had to do to protect innocent people." He proceeded to tell her every act of violence he had ever committed, his life laid bare at her feet. The list was long, the death count high.

When he finished, she said, "You did what you had to do for your job. I don't understand why you're telling me this."

"Because I'm in love with you. I'm completely madly in love with you and I've never felt that way about anyone. With the things I've done, I don't expect that you could ever feel that way about me, but I needed you to know who I am." He looked down.

She stroked his cheek. "Jack, I'm in love with you, too. I spent our first night together memorizing your face: every line, edge, ridge, pore. I knew you were the best thing that would ever happen to me and I was afraid the memory would have to last a lifetime."

"I feel like the luckiest man in the world."

"Jack, let's not worry about all of the details of our pasts. I want to leave the pain behind and just love each other now."

He smiled. "Okay, but maybe I should at least know how old you are and when your birthday is."

"Thirty-eight, and I never cared for holidays, including birthdays."

"Got it. Forty-two and you're the only present I'll ever need." She smiled.

"Let's go to bed," he said.

The next morning, Jack went to work and Tess went home. At the end of the day, they met at his apartment. "I have something for you," he said, holding out a velvet box. "I was passing an antique store and saw it in the window."

She opened the box to reveal a gold heart locket. She beamed and her eyes filled with tears. "Jack, it's the best present I've ever received," she said, putting it around her neck. "I'll wear it every day."

"You have my heart, Tess. My whole heart, forever."

"Promise me something. Don't ever buy me another present again. Nothing could ever be better than this."

"I'm hoping life is long. That's a lot of birthdays, holidays, Tuesdays," he said.

"Flowers. You can always get me flowers if you want to," she replied.

"Which ones are your favorite?"

"White hydrangeas. I never buy them for myself," she said.

They kissed, and then Jack got up and turned some music on. He reached for her hand. "Let's dance."

The second song that played was "All of Me." Two lines into the song, Jack said, "This is our song, I just know it is. Okay, baby?"

She nodded and rested her head on his chest.

They continued to work each day and spend each night together. Thursday night, Tess made eggplant parmesan, which she brought over to share with Jack. While they were eating, he said, "My friends and I go to this place called Shelby's Bar every Friday night. I told them all about you and they really want to meet you. Will you meet us there?"

"Of course," she said. "Tell me about them."

"Joe is in his mid-fifties. We've worked together for about fifteen years. He's a class act. Bobby is young, twenty-nine, and the nicest, most laid-back guy. He joined the Bureau three years ago, but I feel like I've known him forever. His girlfriend, Gina, is an elementary school art teacher. You'll like her."

"Sounds great. What do you think about bringing an overnight bag and staying the night at my place after we hang out with your friends? It's about time you see it. Omar and Clay are coming over for brunch on Saturday and I'm dying for you to meet each other. Will you?"

"Absolutely," he replied.

"Jack, you know how people always talk about all the things they want to do or see in their lifetime? They don't even mention being happy because I suppose they think that's just a given."

"Yeah."

"Happiness has never been a given for me. I guess I pursued other things," she said.

"Me too," he replied.

"But I'm so happy now, with you."

"I love you so much, Tess."

"I love you, too."

ABOUT THE AUTHOR

Patricia Leavy, Ph.D. is an independent scholar and bestselling author. She was formerly Associate Professor of Sociology, Chair of Sociology & Criminology, and Founding Director of Gender Studies at Stonehill College in Massachusetts. She has published over thirty books, earning commercial and critical success in both nonfiction and fiction, and her work has been translated into numerous languages. Her recent titles include *The Oxford Handbook of Methods for Public Scholarship*; *Handbook of Arts-Based Research*; *Research Design: Quantitative, Qualitative, Mixed Methods, Arts-Based, and Community-Based Participatory Research Approaches; Method Meets Art: Arts-Based Research Practice, Third Edition; Fiction as Research Practice; The Oxford Handbook of Qualitative Research, Second Edition*; and the novels *Shooting Stars, Spark, Film, Blue, American Circumstance,* and *Low-Fat Love*. She is also series creator and editor for ten book series with Oxford University Press, Brill | Sense, and Guilford Press, and is cofounder and co-editor-in-chief of *Art/Research International: A Transdisciplinary Journal*. A vocal advocate for public scholarship, she has blogged for numerous outlets, and is frequently called on by the US national news media. In addition to receiving numerous honors for her books, including American Fiction Awards and a Living Now Book Award, she has received career awards from the New England Sociological Association, the American Creativity Association, the American Educational Research Association, the International Congress of Qualitative Inquiry, and the National Art Education Association. In 2016, Mogul, a global women's empowerment network, named her an "Influencer." In 2018, the National Women's Hall of Fame honored her, and SUNY-New Paltz established the "Patricia Leavy Award for Art and Social Justice." Please visit www.patricialeavy.com for more information or for links to her social media.

Printed in the United States
By Bookmasters